TALES
OF THE DON
Charles Sauriol

Edited by Vivian Webb

NATURAL HERITAGE/NATURAL HISTORY INC.

Tales of the Don
written by Charles Sauriol
published by
Natural heritage/Natural History Inc.
P.O. Box 69, Postal Station H
Toronto, Ontario
M4C 5H7
Copyright 1984

Published with a grant in-aid-of publication
from the Ontario Heritage Foundation, Ministry of Citizenship and Culture.

Design and Production   Derek Chung Tiam Fook
Typography   Primetype
Printed and bound in Canada by
T.H. Best Printing Company Limited.

1st Printing – November 1984

Canadian Cataloguing in Publication Data

Sauriol, Charles, 1904-
Tales of the Don

ISBN 0-920474-30-6

1. Sauriol, Charles, 1904-   2. Don River
Valley (Ont.) – History. I. Title.

FC3097.56.S29 1984   971.3'54   C84-098749-8
F1059.5.T686D66 1984

CONTENTS

DEDICATION

To my wife Simonne, my daughters Denise, Monique, Marcelle and son
Claude, and to those many friends French and English speaking who
shared with my family unforgettable and happy hours during our
many summers at the Forks of the Don.

INTRODUCTORY PHOTOGRAPHS

Inside Front Cover Photo:
Don Valley near Pottery Road, 1900.

Bridge over Castle Frank ravine, circa 1880. Photo by the Hon. Alexander M. Ross, Provincial Treasurer.

Original Todmorden Hotel on Broadview Avenue at Pottery Road, circa 1880. (Photo by J.V. Salmon)

"Taylor's Mills, Don Forks about 1890. View toward north from a high hill which was levelled for Parkway". This inscription appears on the back of the photo from the collection of Ted Chirnside of Willowdale, Ontario. The author of "Tales of the Don" affirms that most of the buildings shown in the photo were standing in the 1930's, likewise the orchard in the background of the buildings. However there have been some changes in the scenery, presumably the woods in the upper left hand corner of the photo is the west valley of the Don. The two streams of water in the lower half of the photo do not relate to their present position; these streams are presumably the east branch of the Don and Taylor's creek. Apparently the west branch of the Don does not appear in this photo. It would be to the left of the photo. Nor is the Taylor "upper" paper mill shown in the photo. It stood on the west branch of the Don to the left of the photo. The original scenery at the Forks of the Don and along the east valley of the Don was seriously altered when a railway line was laid along the valley in the early 1900's. Likewise when roads were laid across the valley. Nevertheless the photo is a valuable momento of the Forks of the Don, of the turn of the century.

Original workman's house, occupied by employee of Helliwell Brewery. Later purchased by Rand Freeland, originator of Fantasy Farm on Pottery Road. (Photo: J.V. Salmon)

O'Connor Drive looking east from Pape Avenue, circa 1920. (Photo by Stuart L. Thompson)

Lower Don with Queen Street bridge in background, circa 1920's.

Sugar Loaf Hill close to the Bloor Street Viaduct in 1938. This important geological site was obliterated from the landscape, removed as fill.

INTRODUCTION:

The Way It Was – And Is

In stories I have read about country living there are people who leave their homes and jobs in the city and move, usually to abandoned farms adjacent to wilderness areas, to find independence and, almost invariably, happiness. They make a clean break with their former lifestyles. Their past is in the past. What they seek in the country is acquired at the expense of what they leave behind in the city.

I had no such experience in my search for the rural life. I enjoyed country living but I didn't have to give up the pleasures of the city, my lifestyle or position. I was able to do this due to some unusual circumstances. I acquired four, then five acres of land and a dilapidated dwelling at the Forks of the Don, two miles from my permanent city residence and about four miles from downtown Toronto.

To be able to live in the countryside yet be so close to Toronto is inconceivable today. In the late 1920s the Don Valley stood as a barrier of trees, slopes and flood plain to arrest the city's growth. Bayview Avenue, then a dirt road, ended at the edge of the Valley. Houses and streets straggled eastward from Yonge Street to what later became the burgeoning community of Leaside. Don Mills Road wound northward, girded with stately elms, through the lands of the Meagher, Donlands and other farms. O'Connor Drive did not yet exist.

There were market gardens stretching from Pape Avenue to Woodbine Avenue and beyond. Today the Thorncliffe Plaza stands on what once was farmland, as does Flemington Park. Wexford, Oriole and Agincourt were hamlets I usually reached by bicycle. The Taylor farm at the Forks of the Don has long since been obliterated by housing developments. Today I would have to travel 30 miles or more northward to enjoy the rural and wildwood settings that I found at my door in the '20s and '30s.

The Don Valley was virtually uninhabited when I first knew it. There were a few old houses, some sheds, a few mills, mill dams and the tracings of onetime mill races, abandoned orchards and straggling lilac bushes. These were the most visible signs of a vanished pioneer life.

I was not alone in knowing that a person could live in the country and still be close to the city. Mrs. Wilfrid Davies told me that each spring the Davies family travelled two or three miles from their residence on

Sherbourne Street to spend the summers in the country. In those days the house was surrounded by open countryside dotted with orchards. Mrs. Davies still lives in that summer house, which stands at Hillside Drive South and Broadview Avenue.

Members of the MacLean clan used to meet at Broadview Avenue and Danforth Avenue to be conveyed to Donlands Farm, which was located at Eglinton Avenue and Don Mills Road, far out in the country in those days. Mr. Rupert Edwards told me that Mrs. Edwards felt that their country home, now Edwards Gardens, was too far away from the city for her to enjoy.

Distance means little today but in the '20s it was an important factor, and more so for the generation preceding mine. There used to be halfway houses or inns several miles apart along the main roads. Farmers who could not make the drive by horse and wagon or buggy to the city all in one day would stop at these inns for the night. Todmorden Hotel, demolished to make way for the present Food City, was originally a halfway house.

During the horse and buggy days 20 miles was thought to be the maximum distance a person could travel from dawn to dark. This was partly due to the poor condition of the roads. My assistant's mother, raised in the hamlet of Seagrave, north of Bowmanville, often set out with horse and buggy to visit relatives 20 miles up country. On arrival the horse was stabled for the night and the buggy pulled into a shed built for the purpose. Some of these sheds remain, even in the Toronto region.

When I was a boy it took us as much as two hours travelling to visit Uncle Jim, who lived on Broadway Avenue, east of Mount Pleasant. To get there we travelled by street car, then by radial car up Yonge Street, and finally by foot. Today this journey would be a matter of 15 minutes by car.

My experience in country living so close to home did not come all at once but gradually, over the years, first as a single man, then with my parents, then as a married man with a wife and four children. I was 24 years of age when in 1928 I first took over the property at the Forks of the Don. There, during the first years, I experienced rustic living. I gave up electricity for kerosene lamps, tap water for water hand-pumped from a well, a cozy bathroom for an outhouse, gas or electric heating for a wood stove and coped with other "inconveniences" which at the time I thoroughly enjoyed.

Why did I choose to live this way in the Don Valley when, in the '30s, one could have easily found a rural property or a lakeshore cottage almost anywhere within a hundred miles of Toronto? I probably wouldn't have had to suffer the heartbreak of having my home expropriated 30 years later, as this one was. If I had bought in the Muskokas or someplace like that, the property would have greatly increased in value over the years. But I chose to stay in the Don Valley. Why?

I knew the Valley well, having camped and hiked through it since

Charles Sauriol's cottage on the Don, circa 1920. (Photo by Stuart L. Thompson)

1920 when it was still very much a wilderness. I had developed a love for the Valley and it meant more to me than any other of the places with which I was familiar at the time. So, when I suddenly found that I was in a position to buy land and to set up my stake in this same Valley, the choice seemed clear. The thought of owning property seemed to satisfy all my aspirations. But how was I to know that my plans, from their inception, were on a collision course with the inevitable development of the city? I believed I was building something that would last forever. Had I thought otherwise this book would not have been written.

The urge to locate in the Valley was strong. The Forks of the Don in the '20s and '30s was sylvan, serene and naturally beautiful. Huge graceful elms stood along the river banks and on the flood plain, over which cattle roamed. The lofty walls of Tumper's Hill, otherwise known as Greenbank, commanded a view of the four great ravines which met at the Forks of the Don. Some of the Valley slopes were covered with white pine, long since replaced with the deciduous trees of today. Don Mills Road wound its way along the base of Tumper's Hill then, having spanned the Don, pursued its course up and over the rough bricks of de Grassi Hill on to the wooden trestle bridge, whose planks rattled and shook with the impact of each passing vehicle, one perhaps every ten minutes. Three streams met at the Forks: the West Don, the East Don and Taylor Creek. Huddled in the folds of the Valley and tracing the old course of the East Don were several frog ponds.

The sounds, scenes and scents of nature were everywhere, particularly during the spring. Each April dozens of eastern bluebirds dropped from a sky as blue as their wings to perch for a few moments in a row along my fence wires. I could catch the scent of the balm of Gilead in the evening air when the sad trilling of the American toads echoed along the deserted Valley, a sound so plaintive that it tugged at one's heartstrings. Sometimes I heard a great horned owl and very often the sweet tremolo of a saw-whet owl.

As a young man inclined to the outdoors I felt that the few acres on the Don were a challenge: to make this land productive; to make, through my energies, something out of nothing; to fix up the house; plant shrubs, flowers and fruit trees; to dig a garden and a well. There was nothing sensational in my plans but they satisfied me and have given me many happy memories.

It was also important to me that the Forks of the Don was something to be enjoyed 52 weeks of the year. There was no closing the cottage at the end of the summer for me. Muskoka or other places may have beckoned, but how often could I have gone there? A few dozen times a year, if that. But I could be at the Forks any time I chose, for an hour, a casual visit overnight or for a season. Spring and fall, winter and summer, nature's pages unfolded for me in the parade of the seasons. It could be said that I lived in the Valley because I wanted to and in the city because I had to.

The Forks of the Don was only one part of the Don Valley, a gateway or a portal to what I considered a kingdom of the outdoors, namely the East and West Valleys of the Don. People today who never saw the Valley in the '20s or '30s find it hard to believe that such a large natural area existed at the city's door. But up until 1950 this outdoor haven remained virtually unchanged. Today extensive tracts of land disappear overnight in a welter of construction. Woodlands, wetlands and ravines are obliterated in the flash of a bulldozer's blade. The perspective in my time was one of unchanging beauty. I cannot recall within a span of 30 years the construction of one new house in or near the edges of the lower Don Valley.

To the lover of nature the Valley was a treasure trove. All of the beauties of nature that drew me were within an hour's walk of the Forks. Everything I wanted was there. There were wild flowers in all growing seasons (I identified 125 species of them). Likewise the birds were always close by: the bluebirds in numbers, the phoebe that nested on a ledge over the kitchen door, the wrens for whom we set up boxes and who filled the June days with their warbling, the kingfishers flying up and down the Don from dawn to dusk and the innumerable bank swallows who lived in holes in the river banks across from the cottage.

Even the fallen down remnants of human settlement had their charms. The Taylor and Milne Mills, MacLean's sugar shanty, ruined build-

Forks of the Don looking north from Tumper's Hill.

ings, rambling lilac bushes and ancient apple trees awakened my sense of history and led to a 20-year effort to write a history of the Don Valley. But while history was important to me, it was the contact with nature, and the interpretation of nature, that bound me closest to the Valley. From the 1920s to the 1950s I felt more in harmony with nature than at anytime later in my life. I never lived the outdoor life more intensely than during my early meanderings up the Don. Even though conservation became my career, I cherish these experiences as a tremendous gift.

For 12 years I wrote down my thoughts and experiences in a manuscript which I called "My Seasons". I recorded thousands of observations, which I saw as cameos of nature. It was a delight for me first to live them, then to set them down in words, to be recalled at will.

I remember seeing the full moon break over the pines, spreading its beams of mysterious phosphoresence over the misty shrouds that rose from the river to the flood plain. Breaking the soil in the garden, one of the first jobs of spring, released the fragrance of winter-washed soil. The meadow grasses were blown by the strong June breezes in an endless procession of waves like those of a northern lake. Many an evening I walked to and from the swimming hole as twilight gradually closed down on the day. Then, seated in front of the cottage, I could hear the water flowing over the river stones, and sometimes, just at dusk, the strident call of a whippoorwill.

I have been to many cottages and they all have their charms. But many are confining. Walks may be limited to a single stretch of road. But my kingdom along the Don extended for miles and miles, as open to me as the breezes. Nor was I ever challenged: indeed I never saw a "No Trespassing" sign. I often thought about this and, if I had been asked, I would not have known who owned the woodlands I roamed.

Now, some 60 years after I first set foot in the Don Valley, I think back on what I might have done had I bought property elsewhere in those early years. There remains scarcely a trace of the dwellings at the Forks of the Don that were once important to me. The foundations of the cottage where we spent so many happy summers are buried under the Don Valley Parkway. My second cottage on the other side of the Don, which I called the de Grassi Place, may still be located from a slab of concrete that held the chimney and fireplace. Joe Giguere and I put it there, mixing the cement with river stones. The river bank by de Grassi seems natural with its cover of weed growth, but below this lie the ice-battered remains of old automobiles. More recently loads of broken sidewalk were dumped there to fill in holes gouged out by the flood waters caused by Hurricane Hazel.

But perhaps most intriguing of all to a stranger are the two steel rails protruding through the sandbanks at the river's shore. These rails once served to hold the supports of my cable bridge over the Don. They may well be there forever. My only other handiwork still visible, and which time only improves, is the grove of trees I planted at the rear of the cottage in 1929 or thereabouts. These have now all grown into big trees and are very valuable. They include walnut, butternut, hemlock, yellow birch, maple and ash. They may still be there generations hence.

It is a different Valley today. Much of it is groomed and landscaped. Even the wilderness areas don't seem to be the same. The feeling the Valley once had, of being a wild, isolated place, is gone. Dwellings line the edges of the ravines and, while there are still pockets of wild land and some natural area preserves, hundreds of acres are in effect supervised parks dotted with transplanted trees.

The human use of the Valley has changed too. The hiker has now been replaced by the stroller or the jogger or the skier. In the '20s the Don Valley was invaded each spring by boys whose predominant concern was to set the grass on fire. By April, when their campaign began, the sun had dried out the vegetative cover of the flood plains and adjacent meadows. The fires crept unhindered to nearby woodlands where humus or peat was several feet deep. I have seen acres of a once-fine woodland whose humus was so eaten away as to leave the roots of the trees exposed. And the fires smouldered throughout the summer until finally extinguished by the fall rains. Today the practice of setting the Valley on fire has disappeared and the trees can grow unimpeded. Furthermore, the same schoolboy types who once destroyed the woodlands now plant tens of thousands of seedling trees there each spring.

Another positive change is the planting of pine, spruce and cedar in

Coffee session at DeGrassi cottage, circa 1960.

the protected wetland below the Science Centre. Had these trees been planted without protection in my day, they would have been hacked to pieces.

Some of the Valley traditions have quite disappeared. On Good Friday and Thanksgiving droves of young people used to invade the Valley for a day's outing or a picnic. How this teenage practice came about I do not know but it was certainly popular in the '20s and '30s. Groups of young people used to sit around a bonfire for hours, enjoying a weiner or corn roast. Today there are cement circles to contain the bonfire, with benches or logs for seats, and the firewood is cut for you.

Gone also is the yearly invasion of boys bent on spending their Easter holidays unceremoniously hacking down hundreds of cedar, hemlock and pine trees. These trees were sacrificed in attempts to build shelters, lean-tos and other manifestations of a boy's fancy of what to do in the woods. Some of the finest groves of coniferous trees in the Don Valley disappeared in this way.

Gone too are the scout camps where several troops, each camping in its favourite spot, made good use of the Valley. Gone too is the annual trek of schoolgirls who, in trillium time, came to the Valley and carried away huge bouquets which quickly wilted. These visits depleted slopes once white with trillium petals.

In conclusion let me make a few comments and observations about *Tales of the Don*. Its text was written in draft form during August 1983, re-written and completed by the spring of 1984. The success of *Remem-*

Forks of the Don (West side). Upper paper mill in Foreground. Note Davies house (Centre). The author's cottage beyond smoke from train. Background is present Parkview Hills. Photo 1936.

bering the Don prompted the publisher and I to follow accounts of the early pioneers along the Don with stories from the turn of the century. Stories from my generation and the post-First World War generation are also included.

The stories in *Tales of the Don* fall into four categories. The opening chapters set down local history which for the most part is beyond my personal experience. The second category groups what I call the cottage stories, drawn from my personal experiences when I and my family spent much of our time at the Forks of the Don. The third category consists of bee stories, where they can be suitably identified, and relate to my experiences as a beekeeper. These stories do not conflict with the material used in *A Beeman's Journey*. The fourth category, entitled "Lest Old Acquaintance be Forgot", is a tribute to those people who have played a significant role in my life as companions up the Don.

I felt that many of the chapters should be preceded by a brief synopsis to give the reader useful background information for the events related.

It is my sincere hope that these glimpses into the past will provide the readers of *Tales of the Don* with an appreciation of the community in which they live. The Don Valley has changed, even in the past few years, and we must remember its history before the stories are beyond recall.

CHAPTER ONE

What Was and What Might Have Been

In 1950 a group of citizens of East York joined forces to preserve the Don Valley in its natural state. It was a time when threats against the natural beauty of the Valley were multiplying on every side. Pocket sewage disposal plants were so overloaded that raw effluent was being dumped into the Don River and Taylor Creek. There was a threat of factory development where Todmorden Mills now stands. Wooded slopes and wetlands disappeared under heaps of garbage when they were used as municipal dumps. Trees were felled to provide space for service lines spanning the Valley. Through a lack of regulations, anyone so minded could despoil the woodlands at will.

Although the Valley, generally speaking, was unspoiled, it was obvious that this could not last. The Don Valley Conservation Association (D.V.C.A.) was formed to save the Valley and for ten years mounted one of the most intensive conservation campaigns anywhere. *The Cardinal* recorded many of its achievements, as did the Toronto daily newspapers. Large scrapbooks of clippings indicate the extent of their support of the D.V.C.A.'s efforts.

By 1953 the Association had, among other things, prepared a brochure outlining its concerns, aims and objectives. I found one remaining copy of this brochure. Its language, while flowery, is impressively sincere. It seemed appropriate to include extracts from it with these *Tales of the Don*. Who knows? Without the efforts of the D.V.C.A. the greenbelt may never have matured to what we know today.

I was searching through my files in the course of writing this book and I found a copy of a long-forgotten brochure. It had a picture of a cardinal on the front cover and was entitled: "Presentation of a plan for the protection and beautification of the Don Valley". The brochure was officially presented at Fantasy Farm on October 19, 1953 by the Don Valley Conservation Association. Representatives from municipalities in the Don watershed and members of the general public listened as the D.V.C.A. reviewed in some detail the threats against the Valleys of the Don and recommended measures to correct or meet them. The main areas of concern were: pollution, parks, patrolling and aesthetics – what the Valley could become in terms of a recreational and natural beauty haven.

This brochure is now a collector's item but as I read its yellowing pages I am struck by how clearly those people saw the path of the Valley's development. They recommended that the flood plains be cleared and protected from further misuse, that trunk sewers should be laid to carry effluent to a central point on Lake Ontario. These things have long since been done. They also foresaw that the Don Valley CNR line would carry commuter trains.

The writing is flowery but the facts come out strongly. The D.V.C.A. proved indeed to be a prophet in its own land. Without it, the Todmorden Mills historical village would have been the site of a factory development.

But no one could predict on October 19, 1953 that almost exactly one year later, on October 15, 1954, the room at Fantasy Farm in which the D.V.C.A.'s presentation had been made would be under six feet of water, or that the entire Don Valley would be a lake of flood waters in the wake of Hurricane Hazel. Disasters like that are beyond anyone's ken.

What follows are extracts from the brochure:

POLLUTION

"Sewage pollution in the Don watershed seems to indicate two needs: (1) a pollution authority that requires all plant capacities to keep abreast of population growths. (2) Immediate appropriation of funds to correct the critical overload of Todmorden, Danforth Park and Scarborough sewage plants.

"The latter two of these plants discharge their effluent into what is known as Taylor's Creek. This is a tributary of the Don which has its origin in Scarborough Township and enters the Don north of O'Connor Drive and south of the cement bridge on Don Mills Road. Taylor's Creek at this point is but an open sewer and converts the Don River, from this point south, into the same category. Of considerable distress to many people is the fact that within a few hundred feet of this point is a park and playground area. While modern science still cannot prove it, many authorities believe that the polio virus is present in such water. And our children wade and play in it.

"Of further distress and concern is the problem of stench faced by many residents living adjacent to Taylor's Creek. This odor is so nauseating that it must be experienced to be believed. The ramifications of this condition are both many and obvious. Home owners, many of whom can least afford it, find their property values depressed to the point where they are financially unable to move. Thus the vicious circle is compounded and the toll in terms of physical and mental health must be great indeed. These facts are made more incredible when one realizes that the Don River pollution occurs within the boundaries of the greatest concentration of wealth in our entire country.

"This problem of pollution has been thoroughly surveyed by reputable engineering firms and plans for corrective action have long since been submitted. In view of the fact that rumour indicates present plants must operate for another twenty years before a trunk sewage system is installed, then it certainly follows that present authorities bear a grave responsibility to act with both vigour and efficiency.

PARKS

"As we all know, there are two valleys of the Don, extending from Riverdale Park to the area of Richmond Hill. To set in motion a plan of parks for this vast area is a major undertaking, yet it is the observation of the D.V.C.A. that a start can be made. Indeed a good start has already been made and should be continued.

"Todmorden Park and area to the east of it, is a municipal achievement. The park, with tables furnished by the D.V.C.A., is used by thousands of citizens in summer and winter. It has running water facilities, a Kiwanis Club house and a set of steps reaching it from Don Mills Road. The adjoining woods of Taylor's Bush and Tumper's Mount require very little cleaning up. Here conservation is already at work and will continue if it is not hindered by thoughtlessness.

"The Forks of the Don also has its bright spots. Part of it is privately owned and has been turned into a beauty spot. The Don Valley School of Art has created another attractive area. Some other dwellings of the neighbourhood are dilapidated.

"Don Mills Road will soon be straightened here and with this work will come an opportunity to sod the shoulders of the new highway, to plant trees and, in brief, to follow the practices of good highway care elsewhere. We must not lose the opportunity to get this beautifying work underway as soon as the road straightening is finished.

"The East Valley of the Don, from Don Mills Road to Lawrence Avenue, is an incomparable beauty spot, rich in wildlife, birds, trees and scenery. Its chief requirements are regular patrol, several picnic sites and drinking water. Already East York has built two sets of steps leading to the valley. Eventually much of the area bordering the valley on the North will be built upon, and with this will come the menace of storm sewers linked to the ravines, and the ensuing bad results.

"Already there has been municipal encroachment on the area. The telephone line, followed by the Scarborough water main in their construction caused the ruin of many fine trees, the spoiling of hillsides and the start of erosion pockets. In this area the hydro wires have ruined a fine woodland and have caused erosion on hillsides, which should be planted with small trees.

"The Eglinton bridge will eventually cross the valley. This should be done with as little destruction to adjoining woodlands as possible. The area adjoining Lawrence Avenue East is accessible to the public. It contains hundreds of acres of fine wooded country. Here the Valley is quite unspoiled, quite untouched by any sign of encroachment. Its chief requirements are protection, and the placing of adequate picnicking and hiking facilities.

"The important area of the West Valley of the Don lies in the Milne Creek area, reaching eastwards to the spur line of the CNR Leaside line.

PATROLLING OF THE DON VALLEY
"Several weeks ago, a delegation of citizens approached the Civic Parks Committee and demanded more adequate protection of Blythwood Ravine and Sherwood Park. The delegation complained of vandalism, rowdyism and of attacks on children by perverts.

"The story of this ravine is the story of the whole Don Valley. It is not an uncommon sight to see garbage and refuse dumped indiscriminately in the ravine and along the roads of the Don Valley by people too stupid and selfish to realize they are destroying something that can never be replaced. Altogether too often there have lately been instances of unsavoury and immoral characters molesting, enticing or at the least embarrassing young children in the valley. At various times of the year, notably fall and spring, deliberate vandalism takes its toll of wild-life and natural beauty in the valley. Matches that start grass fires ... axes that in fifteen minutes destroy trees that have taken years to grow ... rifles that kill songbirds already hard put to find shelter ... each such wanton act of senseless destruction hastens the ultimate loss of the one natural recreation area remaining within reach of over a million people.

"It is time that some official action accompany the oft-expressed opinions that the Don Valley is a natural recreation area – that it is essential to public health in city life – that it should be preserved for posterity.

AESTHETIC VALUE OF THE DON VALLEY
"Once tranquil highways, including Don Mills Road, are crowded bumper to bumper with traffic. The fields of yesteryear contain rows of houses. Expansion, we are told, will continue. Zealots of progress foresee the city reaching forty miles on each side; duplicating Chicago and other large centres of the United States in terms of millions of population.

"Fortunately, for the present and future population of Toronto, the Don Valley remains as a winding, green buttress along the east and north ends of the city. In this day of unprecedented commercial development, the Don Valley, close to the city, still remains as it always was, sylvan, serene, beautiful, a wild wood with all of the attributes of a wildwood; birds, flowers, trees, unspoiled places, winding streams, deep-in-the-woods tranquility. A place for the poet, the hiker, the picnicker, the student of nature, the man in quest of a breath of fresh air, moral and physical. Surely no woodland near a great city ever surpassed this Don Valley.

GLANCE INTO THE FUTURE

"May we cast a speculative glance into the future? Toronto has been built up. Scarcely an open lot remains. It has become truly a vast commercial city, but winding its way through the city just as now, is the still-beautiful Don Valley. Many changes have taken place. Weed trees have been removed. Acres of sturdy white and red pine trees border on the trails. Here and there are to be seen a charming picnic site with barbecue, drinking water, benches and happy people sitting about. In the spring of the year, the hillsides are white with trillium. In the trees are heard the calls of countless birds. The clear river has long since lost its pollution to a trunk sewer.

"This future Don Valley has become an organized Provincial Park, the dream of those of us who see it thus today; the delight of those who will follow us. Perhaps in that generation an official tourist guide may read this way:

'The Don Valley, historical and beautiful, Toronto's favourite outdoor recreational area. A preserve for native wildflowers, trees and songbirds. A tribute to those men and women of the early 1950s who had the courage to fight for its preservation.'"

CHAPTER TWO

The Don Valley At Bloor

When Hillside Drive South (across the Valley from Rosedale) was opened up in 1938, I bought a lot on the rim of the Valley for $1,000. The lot extended from Hillside Drive 250 feet down the slope of the Valley.

The house which I built there commanded a view of the Valley which was quite different from what you would see today. Its principal features were the river, the railway, the "half-mile" bridge, the stack and sheds of the Don Valley Brickworks and a collection of sheds, houses and the paper mill building which was later replaced by Todmorden Mills.

I have resided for quite a long time in a house where my living room and bedroom face the west, looking out on the wooded skyline of Rosedale. It has been my good fortune to be able to see the sun set, if I choose to do so, on any day of the year when the sky is clear. I have done this so often that I can tell at a glance the time of year from the position of the sun on the horizon.

Between my home and the setting sun lie my own wooded slopes, Todmorden Mills village, the Don Valley Parkway and beyond that the half-mile railway bridge (though it's not really a half-mile long). The Don Valley Brickworks, caught in a fold of the Valley, abut the ravine where the Belt Line Railway once ran. So my view encompasses both the old and the new and leaves to memory the scenes which in my time have disappeared from the landscape.

When I first stood on my Hillside Avenue lot in 1938 the slope was covered with fruit trees from the once-extensive Taylor orchard. There were no buildings in the Valley, other than those which now make up Todmorden Mills historical village. At night scarcely a light was visible from where I stood. There was still something left of the village of Don Mills. The paper mill was mostly abandoned and parts of it used for Whitewood's stables. There was quite an equestrian community in those days and trail riding was popular in the lower Valley. There were several stables with lofts on the site but they were subsequently destroyed by fire. The Helliwell house, the remains of Helliwell's brewery and the Parshall Terry house were all there, as they are today, but in a state of disrepair.

During the Depression the Don Flats, across the river from the vil-

28

Don Valley Brick Works, 1932.

lage, came into doubtful prominence. In those days freight trains coming into Toronto from the west usually brought with them dozens of indigent men with nowhere else to go. Gradually, however, some of the men began to dig into the Flats and, with pieces of tin, sheet metal and other materials, made habitable shacks which soon dotted an area of the Flats. Cardboard, pieces of wood, anything that could be scrounged, found its way into this bidonville, which would now be considered a disgrace to the city of Toronto. Our generally well-off population of today would be incredulous at the sight of these hundreds of men who, with their bundles of worldly good slung on their shouldeers, made their way to Toronto. The Flats became a gathering place for wanderers from across the country. As I recall, they were basically on their own but were often aided by citizens and shopkeepers, who regularly brought them food, articles of clothing and other items of which they were much in need.

Winter posed a major problem for these men as their shacks could not withstand the frigid blasts of the winter winds. Fortunately the company that owned the Don Valley Brickworks allowed the men to sleep indoors in the kilns. The bricks were baked in ovens fed with four-foot lengths of hardwood. This wood was transported to the Valley in open freight cars and thousands of cords were required to bake the bricks. After the fires had died down, shelter was provided for the men. Without this winter haven, many men would have suffered considerably.

This shack town lasted until the final months of the Depression, when action was taken to close it down. The men were sent off to work camps in the north. All traces of their habitation of the Don Flats were then destroyed.

The Second World War followed in the wake of the Depression. Overnight Canada began to hum with preparations for war. After about a year of the conflict barracks appeared on the Flats across the river from Todmorden Mills, the terrain of which has been altered with the construction of the Parkway. No unauthorized persons were allowed near the camp, which had been built for prisoners of war. Occasionally busloads of prisoners could be seen making their way under guard up Pottery Road to Broadview Avenue.

Within a day of the end of the war the contents of the barracks began to disappear at an alarming rate. The depredations were not considered looting, at least by those involved. Sinks, toilet bowls, electric light fixtures, kitchen equipment, indeed everything that could be carried away was. Then the barracks themselves were attacked and one of them was set on fire. Finally the authorities intervened and what was left of the camp was dismantled. There remains not a trace of it today.

The Don Valley, from the Bloor Street viaduct to the Forks of the Don, was a playground for generations of urchins. This was brought home to me when Toronto radio station CKO personality, John Gilbert, was interviewing me about my book, *Remembering the Don.* Gilbert was born in Cabbagetown and the Don Valley was his playgound. Long before the subway was built, John and his companions discovered that there was a storage room under the bridge that could be reached by climbing one of the viaduct girders. The room was then used as a headquarters for weekends in the Valley, which included swimming in the Don.

After the meeting with John I looked up my manuscript history of the Don and in the chapter "The Sugar Loaf Hill", I came across this verse, which was sung to the tune of "The Blue Bells of Scotland";

> *"Oh where, tell me where did the Yorkville boys swim,*
> *Oh where, tell me where did the Yorkville boys swim,*
> *In the Don at Sandy Point beneath old Sugar Loaf Hill*
> *Near Helliwell's bush and Castle Frank across from Taylor's*
> *Mill."*

This verse, which came from an old newspaper clipping, must have been familiar to hundreds of boys who trekked eastward from Yorkville to the banks of the Don long before John's time. A photograph of Sugar Loaf Hill and the viaduct under construction appears in *Remembering the Don,* p.58.

During that same radio interview John mentioned the huge willows that lined the banks of the Don. These provided great sport for the boys of his time. "We would tie a length of rope to a high branch so that it dan-

30

Prisoners of War. (City of Toronto Archives – James 867.)

gled a few feet above the river," he said. "The trick was to pull the rope as far up the bank as possible, then make a run for the river, hanging on to the rope for dear life."

John also asked me why there were so few white pine left in the Valley. Actually much of the white pine was cut for firewood during the Depression. The Sun Brick Company cut down a large number of trees and used them to build their stables and sheds. Today efforts are being made to replant white pine, now Ontario's emblem tree, in the Don Valley.

The spot where the viaduct now crosses the Don Valley was once a very popular area, as I mentioned in my newspaper column, "Diary of a Conservationist", on June 27, 1955. A woman reader wrote in as follows:

> *"The youngsters of today do not know the fun and pleasure we had winter and summer down old Parliament Hill, now mostly occupied by the viaduct. The winter sledding and sleigh rides and picnics, or noon lunches exploring new roads. We had these places within reach. So much of our beauty is being swallowed up. I hope you and your associates can manage to help teach the younger generation the beauty of the outdoors."*

The *Globe and Mail* of October 24, 1951 featured the viaduct in an article headlined "City Looks Different When Served Country-style". The text was illustrated with a picture of the west end of the viaduct with a market garden in the foreground. The caption reads: "Well within the heart of Toronto in the Don Valley, north of Prince Edward Viaduct, market gardening is a profitable occupation for N. Catalano, who supplies his own fruit and vegetable store."

Below this is another picture of a beekeeper holding a frame of bees. The caption reads: "William McArthur is just down the hill from Rosedale, but to look at his beehives and farm-style house, you'd think you were at least fifty miles from Toronto. He harvests honey and also supplies queen bees to other apiaries."

Today we take the Bloor Street viaduct very much for granted, but such was not the case in 1907. I was leafing through old copies of the *Toronto World* and discovered the following news item from the March 26, 1907 issue. It read: "Bloor Street Viaduct Opposed by Half Dozen. Few property owners trying to thwart the desires of several municipalities. The people of the east are not going to rest and let one or two block progress." That phrase, "block progress", has a familiar ring. It has echoed down the years in the vocabulary of every developer who wanted to replace the natural scene with some project or other. Nevertheless, it is difficult to imagine opposition to the viaduct, considering the use made of it today.

From the Don Station to what is now Todmorden Mills there were many interesting places that were part of the way of life in the early years of the century. John Gilbert asked me if I remembered the sleigh slides in Riverdale Park. I did, but as a small boy. My brother, ten years older, knew much more about them. Before the First World War, Riverdale Park was a popular place. There was the zoo, the Don Flats, which always seemed to be covered with flood water in the spring, and the east slope of the park. In the winter this slope was sectioned off into toboggan and sleigh slides. These, when hosed down, provided swift rides down the slope and across the Flats to the end of the park. Sleigh riding was all the rage and the young men of those days, my brothers included, made their own sleighs. These were well-constructed, held as many as 12 riders and had fancy names. The sleighs were equipped with a length of rope for each rider. These were used to help pull the sleigh up to the top of the slope for another ride.

The slope has long since fallen into disuse for sleigh or toboggan riding. In the '30s downhill skiing became a popular sport. People just went up and down the slope without much attempt at skill. It is amusing to recall that I once went to the park on a Sunday in the mid-thirties, put on my skis and was ready to go down the slope when a park patrolman told me that I couldn't ski on Sunday. It wasn't allowed.

I was never much of a skater but I do recall that many of the amateur hockey clubs played their games on outdoor rinks on the Don Flats. While on the subject of skating, my father and uncles sometimes spoke to me as a boy about skating on the Don. When they came to Toronto from

Author's cousins seated on home-made toboggan in front of 13 Munro Street. Sister Marguerite seated at end of toboggan with Muff. Author second from front. Photo 1912.

Cornwall, Ontario, in the 1880s, the ice on the Don was thick and sound in the winter, except where the springs entered the stream. They told me that on weekends there would be great crowds skating from the bay to the area where the viaduct now stands. My father had a pair of skates which he used first in his home town and then on the Don. The blades turned up at both ends and were set in wood. They were real antiques and I wish that we had kept them.

Then there was the zoo, which everyone in east Toronto knew, and where we went to see the monkeys. And everyone knew where Castle Frank was, although they didn't necessarily know its history. From there "up valley" meant the half-mile bridge, Taylor's Mill, the Brickworks and later, the viaduct. I didn't know what lay beyond these points until I joined the Scouts in 1920.

I suppose there are men in Toronto today who could tell dozens of tales of their escapades up the Don. My elder brothers had a few scrapes of their own, which often brought a policeman to our door. One of my business contacts told me years ago that as a youngster he and several other boys broke into a boxcar on a siding near the viaduct and removed several sticks of dynamite. The gang and the dynamite ended up near the north wall of Taylor's Mill. Something happened and a wall of the mill blew out. The boys were never caught and the matter remained a deep secret until many years later, when my acquaintance met one of the

Top of Woodbine Avenue, 1928. Left to right, Charles Brindamour who taught author to ski, Provincial policeman by name of Richards who helped form East York Ski Club and the author.

owners of the mill. By then everyone was able to laugh at the story. The mill manager remarked, at the end of the evening, "So that's how the wall blew in! I often wondered."

CHAPTER THREE

The Taylor House

The following chapter relates a unique experience which, after approximately 40 years, brought historical research and beekeeping together in an unusual way.

While writing my as yet unpublished "History of the Don Valley" in the '30s, I "discovered" the John Taylor house, built in 1826. It had survived five generations of the Taylor family. I took snapshots of the dwelling for my records. The house was later demolished and in time I forgot about it.

However, in 1981 a series of circumstances brought me back to the very location of the Taylor dwelling. I did not realize at the time that my newly-established bee yard was located on the very site of the Taylor's pioneer home.

I felt the story was well worth recording.

In the early 1930s I spent some time exploring the area between Pottery Road and Beechwood Drive, which was much wilder in those days than it is at present. At the time I was writing a history of the Don Valley and I came across some interesting things about the Pottery Road – Beechwood Drive area in so doing. Writing a history of a valley, or rather two valleys, as with the Don Valley, is a major task. Even in a comparatively small area the historian soon finds himself immersed in an endless chain of fact and speculation.

Pottery Road was so named because a man by the name of Burns made pottery on a site close to the Canadian National Railway line where it crosses Pottery Road. There are still fragments of pottery strewn around the slopes of the Valley in this area. Near the site of Burns' pottery was one of the largest white elm trees I had ever seen. It must have been all of 300 years old when I saw it in the 1930s, a real giant.

During my historical research I learned that John Taylor, the pioneering Taylor, had built an unusual medieval-style house in the Don Valley. I set out to find it. Even today the reader can retrace my steps by walking east along the trail that flanks the Don River from Pottery Road to the middle paper mill, which is still in use. I learned that there had once been another mill on this site: Major David Secord had built a saw mill there in 1815, which may have induced the Taylors to locate their paper mill on the same site. They used the mill race built by Secord, which is still in evidence today.

I located the Taylor house and this is what I wrote about it in 1930 or thereabouts:

"*A few hundred feet east of the building of the Don Valley Paper Co. [Taylor middle mill], and within sight of the Leaside bridge [built in 1927], stands an odd-looking unpainted clapboard dwelling with a peaked roof. Built across the front of the house, from the second storey and jutting beyond it in the form of a portico at the south end, is a ten-foot by twenty-foot clapboard oblong. This billboard in miniature is decorated with three inverted "V's" made of wood. It is this strange banner that gives the house its unusual appearance. The dwelling stands on a small plateau well up from the river bank, and in the shelter of the south wall of the Valley. It seems buried in seclusion; the hen coops, the rambling shed, the garden plot, the vagrant, gnarled apple trees are reminiscent of pioneer days. One has the impression of coming suddenly face to face with a scene from the past.*

"*This house, erected in 1826, has survived five generations of the family of the man who built it. It has miraculously escaped the hundred dangers which beset a wooden abode in a new country.*

"*The John Taylor house, for such it is, also has the distinction of preserving a design of construction which can be traced back to the English medieval house. R.J. Jones, a student of the University of Toronto who researched the origin of the English medieval house, obtained these notes from a writing by Hugh Brown on the subject.:*

The medieval method of carrying the ends of the ridge, appears to have been based on the coupled-rafter method ... employing at either end a pair of stout beams like extra large rafters, leaning against each other and firmly secured at their tops upon which rested the end of the ridge-piece ... a right piece of construction in the form of a triangular prism around which the house could be built..."cruck method of construction".

"*If a bowed tree could be found and split up the middle, the two halves, set in contra position, would give excellent support for the ridge piece and give a section much more like that of a house than had been*

36

Parshall Terry house in natural state April 1944. Ridge in background is presently iden-
tified with Hillside Drive S. East York. Top right, Taylor House and building where Taylor
paper bags were made.
The Terry house has been restored and is part of the present Todmorden village.

> *the case with the old tent-like structure ... such curved*
> *beams are called 'crucks' and houses built on the*
> *cruck principle were common throughout the coun-*
> *try during the Middle Ages, continuing to be built in*
> *the north and Midlands until the 18th Century ...*
> *when these crucks were placed in walls filled with*
> *wattle and daub, etc., they formed wall "bays".*

"I took a snapshot of the Taylor house at the time but regretfully have
not been able to find it. No doubt there are other pictures of the house
that will some day be added to our collections to give us a better idea of
what was probably the most unique dwelling in the entire Don Valley."

Being occupied with other matters I turned my back on the Taylor
lot for more than 50 years. In the course of time the wilderness scene I
have described was altered by the building of the Woburn Degreasing
Company's factory to the east of the paper mill. Then chance – or was
it fate? – brought me back to the same site – but not for historical
research.

Beekeeping was one of my primary interests when I lived in the Don
Valley. In the fall of 1980 my fortunes as a beekeeper were at low ebb. My
once thriving apiary at the Forks of the Don had disappeared in the wake

of expropriation. My attempts to continue beekeeping four miles north of Tweed, while successful for several years, finally ended when a bear cleaned out the hives. John Jones, whom I had helped with his Don Valley bee yard, was forced to close down his operation. Then I helped a beekeeper near Stouffville for a while but the area was poor in bee plants and the apiary was moved to Brampton. Beekeeping is a hobby that gets into the blood and I began to miss it badly.

Many years had passed since I did my historical research on the Don Valley but I continued my walks in the Valley. This was made more convenient when the Metropolitan Parks Department began to build bicycle and foot trails all through the Don Valley ravines, from Riverdale Park to many miles north. In order to link the walkway, an arrangement was made with Bate Chemical, Polyresins Division, to forego a strip of land owned by the company adjacent to the Valley slope. In so doing the company found it necessary to fence in two acres of land with an eight-foot chainlink fence at a cost of $17,000. Few people know of the company's generosity and its public-spirited gesture.

Fifty years is a long time and I had completely forgotten that I had once rambled through this same area when it looked much different. The Don Valley Flats are covered all summer long with acres of field flowers, ranging from Japanese bamboo to goldenrod. Many times during my walks I would pause by the chainlink fence, gaze at the wilderness beyond and say, "I would give anything to be able to keep a few beehives here, just for the fun of it, and to try my hand at creating a bee garden ... "

This went on for a long while. Then, with a "nothing ventured, nothing gained" attitude I wrote the company manager to inquire if the company would entertain a proposal to keep a few hives on the premises. I knew I was on safe ground with respect to the bees: the Polyresins Division made products that were no threat to bees. Actually the bees simply ignored the vegetable oils that went into the company's products. I knew this because Jones kept ten hives for as many years a stone's throw or so from the company holdings. His hives produced yearly crops of a very fine quality honey.

Matters worked out far better than I had expected. The manager, Mike Stasko, invited me to bring my hives down anytime. The company was ecstatic that finally someone had come on the scene who could make use of the wild land, and a very good use at that. So the lot became a public relations vehicle, supporting bee research. This was the start of what has proven to be a highlight in my career as a beekeeper. The Bate bee experiences from the fall of 1980 until the spring of 1984 have all been set down in *A Beeman's Journey* and I will try to avoid any repetitions. However it is a very wonderful story and perhaps an unusual one in this way.

After I had settled on the lot, with my apiary in full production, I began to look around at my surroundings. One day it all came to me in

Davies house (formerly Taylor house) Forks of the Don, 1938. Location is now E.T. Seton park.

a flash; my bee yard was virtually on top of the John Taylor house which I had explored more than 50 years before. The wild land owned by Bate Chemical was part of the Taylor property.

The description of the Taylor property I had written in the '30s fitted the site perfectly. Obviously the small plateau on which the house had stood was well above the Don and its flood waters. This plateau was indeed within the shelter of the south wall of the Valley. There are other reminders, such as the pieces of brick and other material I turned up with my spade. It seems incongruous in the face of the development that has occurred over the years that part of the Don Valley is returning gradually to a wilderness state, largely because some of it is privately owned. The Taylor mill race is still visible and the land between the lot and the river bank is covered with trees, to which I have added several hundred seedling red pine.

However it was the Valley slope, also owned by Bate, beyond the walkway that attraced my attention as a wilderness area. On occasion, when caught up with my bee work, I would explore the wooded plateaus and hidden folds of the Valley. It was a delight to see that several species of plants which I did not expect to see were growing as they might have grown elsewhere a hundred years before.

When Ernest Thompson Seton, the great author and naturalist, roamed the Valley the Flats hereabouts were called the buttonwoods because of the many sycamore trees whose seeds had been blown into Ontario from the Ohio Valley. I recall observing some of these trees near the Leaside bridge which were veritable giants.

The visitor may observe, when driving down Beechwood Drive, a stretch of the Valley that indeed reflects nature's grandeur. Here are hundreds of magnificent trees, predominantly sugar maples. I can only hazard a guess as to what miracle saved these trees from destruction. The towering maple, the ash, basswood, pine and hemlock are reminiscent of the Don Valley's heyday. These Valley slopes should be seen in spring when the maples light them with the pale lemon yellow of their April flowers. And, when the brilliant hues of the maples' autumnal regalia of red, crimson, scarlet, brown, yellow and orange blanket the Valley. John Lea would have described it as a "temple not made with hands". Nature's beauty is very visible to those who have the eyes to see it.

CHAPTER FOUR

In Memory of Ernest Thompson Seton
(1860–1946)

I am often overcome by a wave of nostalgia for the good old days of the Don Valley, when it was frequented by Ernest Thompson Seton. Seton was undoubtedly the best known person ever associated with the Don Valley. I knew about Seton from early boyhood days through his book, Two Little Savages, *a book based in part on Seton's experiences as a youth in the Don Valley.*

Mr. Seton graciously responded to my requests for more information about Mud Creek ravine, later known as the Belt Line, where he built his cabin. We corresponded for several years. This chapter also recalls two of Seton's bird stories written from experiences in the Valley. I have added some of my own observations about raccoons, which Seton predicted would disappear from the Don Valley. Of course the opposite has occurred; raccoons have multiplied at a rate no one expected. The increase in population is a result of changes in the Valley's ecology.

For example, in Chris Strong's day (see Remembering the Don, *pages 46-48), raccoons lived in large trees. Now that there are fewer "coon trees", they have taken up alternate living quarters, such as chimneys and sheds. In my 16 years in the Tweed district I have yet to see a raccoon. They are most certainly there, but in normal populations which are supported by the natural resources of the area.*

Seton's nephew, Stuart L. Thompson, and his wife Eleanor, who resided in Leaside, were my personal friends. Stuart and Uncle Ernest always went tramping the Valley on Seton's visits to Toronto. Once, Stuart told me, they stood on Governor's Bridge looking south. "It was over there," Ernest said, indicating the ravine wall. This was the place he knew as Glenyan and he was pointing out the site of his cabin.

It was through my efforts that a section of the Don Valley Metropolitan Toronto Parks system was named "Ernest Thompson Seton Park". The name has regretfully been shortened and the park is referred to as "E.T. Seton Park".

In my library there is an old, tattered book inscribed, "Wishing Leo a Merry Christmas" and dated 1913. It was a present from one of my sisters to an older brother. The book is entitled *Wild Animals I Have Known,* by Ernest Thompson Seton. I kept it all through the years because it is one of the few books based in part on the Don Valley. Seton was a world-renowned author and one of the great naturalists of modern times. I have selected two stories from *Wild Animals I Have Known* as being appropriate for this book; namely, the story of "Silverspot", the crow, and "Redruff", the story of a Don Valley partridge.

As a boy Seton lived on Howard Street, which ran off Parliament at Bloor. I took a picture of the house in which his family resided, since demolished. Seton in his early days haunted the Don Valley and many of his writings were based on these explorations. His best known book on the Don was *Two Little Savages.*

Silverspot really lived in the Don Valley, north of Toronto, and was killed in 1889 between the Sugar Loaf Hill and Castle Frank by a great horned owl. In his story Seton relates:

> *"Old Silverspot was a leader of a large band of crows that made their headquarters near Toronto in Castle Frank, which is a pine-clad hill on the north-east edge of the city. It was in 1885 that I first noticed this old crow. My windows overlooked the ravine. An old descendant told me, "that there old crow has been a 'flying up and down this ravine for more than twenty years.'"*

Seton gives a detailed account of Silverspot and the doings of his band of crows. They lived in the neighbourhood of Sugar Loaf Hill, Castle Frank and Rosedale Ravine, all actually on the outskirts of Toronto in 1885.

Seton's account of the crows' habits is a classic of observation. Then, in 1893, Silverspot disappeared. A great horned owl was seen in the woods.

> *"Two days afterwards, at dawn, there was a great uproar among the crows . . . all around were the signs of a struggle, but the poor crow had been dragged from his perch at night . . . I turned over the remains, alas it was 'Silverspot'. . . The old nest on the Sugar Loaf is abandoned now. The crows still come in spring-time to Castle Frank, but without their famous leader, are dwindling. Soon they will be seen no more in the old pine grove in which they and their forefathers had lived and learned for ages."*

The story of Silverspot was confirmed in a letter which Mr. Seton sent to me on March 22, 1933. It read in part: "From the head of Sherbourne Street, leading north-westerly, there is a great viaduct today. As this

Rock on Castle Frank Hill where Seton found silverspot.

crosses the ravine of Castle Frank it passes nearly over a huge granite boulder about five feet high and ten wide. It was alongside of this boulder that I found the body of Silverspot, the King Crow, after he had been murdered by the Owl in the late '70s."

Writing in *The Cardinal* in June 1953 I said, "The upper half of a large boulder protrudes from the plateau a short distance south of the site of Castle Frank. By rubbing charcoal over the face of this boulder, I was able to detect the figures 1796 and to the left of this date, the letters 'A.H.M.O.' and 'Y.O.C.U.' "

The date 1796 inscribed on the granite boulder has some historical significance. It coincides with the period during which Governor Simcoe was involved with the building of Castle Frank: "I mean that Castle Frank shall be considered as part of the 5000 acres," he wrote on July 20, 1796.

In the course of events Sugar Loaf Hill disappeared, used as fill for the Don Valley Parkway. But the crows did not disappear, as Seton predicted. They are still with us and range the Don Valley from early or mid-March. For all we know they may still be fearful of a great horned owl, as on occasion one comes to the Don Valley. A great horned owl once came as close as the apple tree by my study overlooking the valley.

Seton began his story of Redruff, the Don Valley partridge, this way: "Down the wooded slope of Taylor's Hill, the mother partridge led her brood, down toward the crystal brook that by strange whim was called

Mud Creek." He then tells how the mother partridge trained her brook to survive the perils of hunters and winter. "Cuddy" is the villain of the story:

> "'Cuddy' lived in a wretched shanty near the Don, north of Toronto [Bloor Street at the time]. He had no wealth, no taxes, no social pretensions and no property to speak of. His life was made up of little work and as much outdoor life as he chose. He considered himself a true sportsman because 'he was fond of hunting and took a sight of comfort out of seeing the critter hit the mud when his gun fired.' The neighbours called him a squatter and looked on him merely as an anchored tramp. The lawful season for hunting partridge began September 15th [in Seton's time] but there was nothing surprising in Cuddy's being out a fortnight ahead of time."

Eventually the character of Redruff, one of the chicks, emerges. Redruff became a Don Valley partridge of note and Seton found much to write about him. Redruff's quest for food led him from Taylor's Hill to Rosedale Creek and Castle Frank Ravine.

Thump, thump, thump, thunder r r r r r r r r r r m m m." Who with woodland property in Southern Ontario has not heard this familiar yet inspiring sound, particularly on a warm sunny spring day? It is the drumming of a partridge, or grouse, as they are generally known. I have heard it often on my property near Tweed. The sound is produced by the partridge beating its wings against a log. A fairly successful imitation may be produced by tapping one's hand quickly on the top of a sofa armrest.

Redruff managed to elude Cuddy but, like Silverspot, the crow, he fell prey to a great horned owl. Seton dramatized the incident this way:

> The wind blew down the valley from the north. The snow horses went racing over the wrinkled ice, over the Don Flats, and over the marsh toward the lake, white, for they were driven snow, but on them scattered dark, were riding plumy fragments of partridge ruffs – the famous rainbow ruffs. They rode on the winter wind that night, away and away to the south, over the dark and boisterous lake, as they rode in the gloom of his mad moon flight, riding on and on until they were engulfed, the last trace of the last of the Don Valley race. For now no partridge comes to Castle Frank. Its woodlands miss the martial spring salute, and in Mud Creek Ravine, the old pine drum log, since unused, has rotted in silence away."

Seton was right; the partridge disappeared from the lower Don Valley. They liked to establish themselves in protected woodlots or natural areas. What a pity we have been deprived of their heartwarming presence which, along with the drumming of woodpeckers, is one of the delightful sounds of spring. Pheasants have been "planted" in the Valley at various times and we sometimes see them strutting about.

As for Cuddy, I have often wondered who he was. I knew about Cudmore House at the top of Bayview Avenue, overlooking the Valley to the south, and thought that perhaps "Cuddy" was an abbreviation of Cudmore, but I doubt it. The Cudmore house was a rather fine country residence and suggested a measure of prosperity that could not be related to Cuddy and his shack.

Much of Seton's rambling country in the lower Valley has changed today beyond recognition. Taylor's Hill and Mud Creek ravine have been altered by the Don Valley Brickworks. This makes it all the more important that we preserve the fragments that have been left to us from its heyday, as priceless fragments of our past.

James Polk, in his *Wilderness Writers,* informs us that Seton's family first lived on a farm near Lindsay after emigrating to Canada. The family later moved to Toronto. Ernest, homesick for the Lindsay woods, spent much of his free time roaming through the glens and ravines on the outskirts of Toronto. In the 1870s areas like Queen's Park, the Rosedale hills and the Don Valley were still virgin wilderness.

The following extract from *Wilderness Writers* refers to Seton's Glenyan:

> *"On Saturdays however, Ernest forgot school work and went exploring the country north of the city. One day, when he was fourteen years old, he came upon a beautiful, thickly wooded glen hidden in one of the ravines. There was a clear brook running through it, and only the chatter of birds and squirrels broke the hushed silence. With great care he built a small cabin near the brook and for more than a year spent every Saturday there, trying to live up to his own ideal of Indian life... Here in his private paradise he spent some of the happiest days he had ever known, collecting wildflower specimens."*

Seton wrote about another Don Valley raccoon called "Wayatcha", or some similar name. Although I read the story many years ago, I have failed to relocate it so must rely on memory. In substance, however, Seton said that the Don Valley raccoons would disappear. He once wrote, in 1885 or thereabouts: "If his hollow tree and himself should meet their doom, it means the final conquest of the final corner of our land by the dollar and its devotees." While many Don Valley coon trees have disappeared, the Valley woodland remains and with it, the raccoons. Hunting was the greatest threat to raccoons in Seton's day. Hundreds of

Cudmore House at top of present Bayview Avenue. Photo circa 1928.

Davey the pet raccoon.

raccoons were hunted by such men as Chris Stong, "the greatest coon hunter of all time", and his little dog Pepper. Today hunting is no longer allowed and raccoons have been multiplying at a sensational rate. Which brings me to the subject of a Don Valley raccoon called Davey.

The Fall 1952 issue of *The Cardinal* carried on its front cover a picture of Bob Speakman, a patrol officer for the Don Valley Conservation Authority, holding two tiny raccoons in his hands. In the background a lad is feeding a third tiny raccoon with an eye dropper. Speakman had found the abandoned family and asked if I would like to raise one as a pet. This is how Davey, the Don Valley raccoon, became a part of this story.

In the 1950s I still owned property at the Forks of the Don and promptly built spacious quarters there for young Davey, but only after raising him at home to early adulthood. In no time at all he was running up and down the street or riding in the back of the car or looking out at traffic or pedestrians. All this was something of a sensation in our neighbourhood. In the beginning it was great fun to watch Davey romp in the kitchen, but not for long. In seconds he could locate potatoes, flour, carrots and a few other items and scatter them. My wife promptly put her foot down and forbad Davey's presence in the kitchen.

Eventually he was transferred to his Don Valley quarters and travelled back and forth to the cottage with me. Davey also became a hiking companion. He would prance or trot alongside me as I walked along the railway or as soon as I made for the woods, as busy as a kite in a high wind. He never stopped poking about or investigating. He was constantly on the lookout for whatever interested him, and everything did interest him.

Although we rambled for hours, Davey always stayed in sight. At the cottage he developed a few habits that were interesting to watch. For example, when I mowed the lawns with a hand-powered mower, Davey would trot alongside. When I turned, he turned to follow me back up the driveway or across the lawn.

When we arrived at the cottage Davey would spend an evening romping with me. But when I was ready to collar him, he would promptly disappear under the veranda and resist all attempts to return him to his quarters. One evening he exhausted my patience. Turning on my heel, I shouted, "If that's what you want, you're on your own." But no sooner had I started walking down the driveway than Davey came out of hiding and trotted alongside me. It became a regular game. All I had to do was walk away and out he would come. Then I would merely reach down, pick him up and return him to his pen.

My family enjoyed his antics no end, particularly his passion for ice cream. I never saw anything like it. To begin with, ice cream was cheap in those days. On the way to the cottage I would stop at Donlands Dairy and ask to have two thermos jars filled. These were the widemouth, picnic-type jars generally used for soup. At five cents a scoop, I had the jars filled quite often. We taught Davey to hold a cone and he became quite skilful at eating the ice cream we topped it with.

But there came a time, despite my efforts to be kind to him, when Davey became restless and, at times, almost wild. He started chewing his tail and this told me something. He wanted to be free, to roam the Valley and catch crayfish and be done with the gentle life for good. So one evening we went for a walk along the stream, back to a wilderness area full of springs, hidden places and great large trees. Davey kept on going and I made no effort to bring him back. That was the last I saw of him. The moral of the story is, leave wildlife alone where it belongs. I never tried to raise another raccoon.

Up until the 1960s raccoons were respectable, law-abiding types with a folksy, country manner. They roamed the Valley at night looking for tidbits such as crayfish, minnows, frogs, toads, insects and whatever else raccoons fancy. There were acres of corn planted along the edges of the Valley in my day. Some of the outside rows were planted in sweet corn to keep the coons away from the main plantings. The coons lived a rural life and when the cold days of winter approached, they merely went to a great old basswood or sugar maple tree and piled in, sometimes half a dozen or so all together, and remained there until spring. It was all so orderly, so romantic – and so inspiring to the nature writers.

Raccoons were still a curiousity then, still creatures of the wild. Raccoons today have a lifestyle quite different from their forebearers. I often ponder about the conditions that have transformed the raccoon of this day from a denizen of the wild into a garbage-raiding nuisance who sets up his den in a fireplace, as in my case. One raccoon recently had the effrontery to steal a hamburger from my neighbour's hands in broad daylight. The raccoon today treats humans with disdain and hurries along the street, from one house to the other, unmindful of their presence. A recent feat of theirs has been to chew my marigolds. To cap it all, the neighbourhood coons raise an infernal din at the bottom of my lot in the moonlight. No garbage may be set out until morning, for these modern raccoons merely tip the containers over and roll them until the covers come off, an easy feat indeed to coons who have learned to unscrew the tops of Coca Cola bottles.

At a time when I felt that I was still master of the situation, I bought a "have a heart" trap. I caught raccoons in it, as well as skunks and squirrels. It was pretty exasperating, however. The next morning I would transport the cage and coon up-Valley, only to learn that the captive, finding the trap comfortabe, had to be pushed out.

I suppose that the raccoon is something we are going to have to live with. In settling the edges of our valleys we have brought untold opportunities to coons to help themselves to our garbage, and they do. The coon's greatest enemy, a man with a gun, has been eliminated. The Parkway and extension have cut into the raccoon's habitat and forced the critters to over-use the land left in a natural state. Then there are the trees. There are still many coon trees in the Valley but the population has far outstripped them, hence the recourse to chimneys and other substitute shelters.

Raccoons are not easily dissuaded. It cost me $100 to have my chimney wired at the top. All for nought because the covering was removed deftly and the coons used the chimney as before. And I left them alone, as we use a downstairs fireplace. A good thing because, as I learned, the coons would have removed the top chimney bricks, one at a time, had it been necessary to do so.

One evening late in June I was walking over the Leaside bridge and paused to look down from one of the buttresses. There below me were five raccoons walking in a file: the parents and three half-grown cubs, very sedate, very organized, setting out for a night on the town.

I make no predictions about what will happen, or if some day we will still be overrun with raccoons. Meanwhile, I am on the lookout for a few wooden apple barrels. When I find them they will be suitably wired to the trees on my lot. It is my guess that they will become as popular as abodes for the coons as starter houses to young families in a new subdivision.

I don't go wandering up the Don Valley on a moonlit night like I used to years ago with Eric La Trobe, but memories of those nocturnal outings

Ernest Thompson Seton House, Harvard Street, 1940.

still filter through. I think of a sharp frosty October night when we would suddenly stop and listen to the sharp cries coming from huge maples off in the woods, where the country cousin raccoon lived out its life on a few dozen acres just about where Maclean's sugar shanty stood. Ah, those far off days when raccoons were raccoons.

CHAPTER FIVE

The Way of the Way Freight

I am one of those fortunate individuals who lived in the era of the steam locomotive, the giants of steam. In my day, trains could take you almost anywhere on the continent. I lived close to a railway line that ran up the East Valley of the Don so my recollections of train travel, where a shrieking locomotive whistle was invariably part of the event, are surrounded by other memories of a facet of life that has since disappeared. The CNR and CPR lines in east Toronto were on steep grades. Each night we would hear the panting and chugging of huge locomotives trying to make the grade.

For many years every morning at 8 o'clock a way freight left the yards and made its way up the Valley, passing my cottage. It was a workhorse, pulling a string of freight cars which were dropped off here and there between Richmond Hill and Washago. I determined to ride on a way freight, to travel seated in a caboose, just once and did.

I had friends at CNR who arranged the trip for me on the understanding that when I bought my ticket and handed it to the conductor of the way freight, I was on my own: the Company bore no responsibility for my presence on the train. Climbing aboard that caboose at the old Don Station and proceeding up Valley was one of the most delightful experiences I have ever had. It is as fresh in my mind today as when it happened 36 years ago. We travelled through fields that all too soon were eaten up by the suburbs of Toronto. The story of my journey, a salute to a way of life that has disappeared, was written from caboose No. 1360.

The Canadian National line skirted the Don River across from my cottage and I had a commanding view of the trains, freight and passenger, as they appeared from under the railway bridge at de Grassi Hill on Don Mills Road. It got so that I knew the schedules of every train. I was so used to them that they never awakened me at night, even though I slept outdoors on the veranda.

They were powerful locomotives in those days. I could hear them puffing and panting as far away as Riverdale Park. There were trains that ran to Muskoka; "the bug" that was used on the Beaverton run and that always came down the Valley on Saturdays a few minutes before 5 o'clock; the Winnipeg passenger train, a sleek monster that lumbered past the cottage about 8 o'clock in the morning and which one morning ran into Walter Mayne's flock of geese when the gander did not have sense enough to keep off the track. Walter had a busy time of it that morning, plucking 16 or more freshly killed geese. Then there was No. 1360., the workhorse of way freight that every morning steamed by my lookout on its way to Washago.

The way freight was an interesting little train with its assorted boxcars. Its purpose was to pick up and drop off freight cars en route. I decided one day that I would like to ride the way freight, just to know what was going on. This was not easy because passengers were not allowed on freight trains. But I had connections at CNR and was given permission to ride in the caboose.

In due course I bought a ticket, just as for any other train. The conductor of the way freight collected my ticket when I boarded the train at Don Station about 8 o'clock in the morning. As usual I was lucky. The weather on that August 18, and indeed the following day, was beautiful. As the train steamed out of the Don Station I stood on the steps of the van. What a thrill it was to round the bend by de Grassi bridge and to see my wife, her father, the children and my parents waving as the train went by.

It was a long day, full of priceless memories. Imagine crop-laden fields north of Oriole. Today the area is built up as solid as can be. I remember sitting behind the engineer as the train skirted the east shore of Lake Simcoe and gathering watercress from a clear stream while the train stood on a siding waiting for a passenger train to roll by. When a member of the crew delayed shutting off the water to douse the coal at Richmond Hill and swamped the engineer, I came away with my vocabulary richer for the experience. No. 1360 depended greatly on the quality of coal that it took on. Sometimes there was trouble getting up a proper head of steam and water had to be mixed with the coal. Also, as the engineer told me, Richmond Hill was the highest point of land on the journey and from there northwards it was down grade all the way.

The ride in the way freight was a tremendous experience. I had a copy of Fenimore Cooper's *The Last of the Mohicans* with me and read it during the rest stops, of which there were many.

It was late in the evening when we reached Washago and I was served on of the best Irish stews I ever tasted. It was in a restaurant run by a Frenchman that catered to the railway staff. These men required good food and lots of it. The Frenchman met the challenge for something like 35 cents a meal. "Those were the days," as Archie Bunker would say. I put up at a boardinghouse a few streets from the Gravenhurst Station, had breakfast there and was back in the caboose at 7 o'clock the next morning. We steamed out of Gravenhurst with only the locomotive and caboose. Pickups were made along the way.

Naturally I got to know the crew well and from then on, whenever No. 1360 was due to pass the cottage, the family all rushed out to the veranda to wave to the crew. And the crew stood by the windows of the train to wave back to us! Here is the story, just as I wrote it at the time.

"I spend a great deal of my time travelling by train and enjoy the best that railways have to offer. Yet here I am, riding the caboose of the Bala Way Freight which operates between Don Station and Gravenhurst.

"Why, one might ask? Well, perhaps it is became of an innate curiousity to learn more about the other fellow and how he makes his living. Then again, I wanted to see something firsthand of the freight end of railroading.

"I selected this way freight for my experiment because it is unhurried: a sturdy little engine (No. 1360) pullings about 15 cars, something entirely divorced from the roar and rush of giant locomotives and their strings of 60 cars.

"By the way, I warn you that anyone who has the aspiration to travel in the caboose must be prepared to travel a long way in the matter of securing permission. It just isn't done for the man on the street, unless there is a particularly good reason for wishing to undertake the journey.

"I boarded the freight at Don Station. The way freight twists and winds along the serpentine track of the Valley. The old landmarks go by, one by one: Riverdale Park, Castle Frank, Sugar Loaf Hill, the Brickworks, the half-mile bridge, the paper mill, the Forks of the Don. Then the scene changes to one of park-like woodlands and the unspoiled stream of the upper Don Valley. Most noticeable of all are the conservation signs, "Don't Cut Trees", at intervals along the right of way.

"To one who has never been in a caboose, or van as it is also called, the experience comes as a surprise. The inside of this one is panelled with hardwood. It is clean and cozy. Three folding beds line the walls. It is living, bedroom and sitting room all in one. A potbellied stove and ice box and sink are essential equipment.

"The eyes of the caboose are the windows of the cupola, an elevated observation tower which protrudes above the roof of the caboose and is built in at the rear end of the cab. Sliding windows communicate readily with the outdoors. The cupola is glassed in on all four sides. Here is the best way to see the countryside.

"The train moves heavily across the crop-laden lands of the area north of Oriole. There are six cars of gravel and stone in the load which keeps the gait of No. 1360 down to about ten miles an hour.

"First switching takes place at Richmond Hill. The engine cuts off from its freight cars, then annexes a further burden of empties to be dropped off at other stations further along the way. As part of my privilege, I enjoyed the novelty of moving with the landscape to the jogging

Canadian Northern line through Taylor Bush in 1920's.

gait of the slightly swaying engine, perched on an engine cab seat the while.

"I have a healthy respect for railroaders who, as I know them, are fine fellows. The crew of No. 1360 was no exception to the rule. On each freight there is a crew of five. The engineer who carries the nickname of "Hogger", the fireman or "Tallow Pot", the brakeman or "the Shack", the conductor or "the Brains" and the end brakeman of "Tail End Shack". The caboose is also called "the crummie".

"At Vandorf, the way freight pulls into a siding and allows No. 55 passenger train to speed on its way to North Bay. A half hour later, No. 103 freight sweeps by, clippity, clippity, clip, and once again our multi-merchandise convoy is all alone on the rails. In the meantime the needs of the crew are not forgotten and "Tail End Shack" has set before us an appetizing meal of deep-browned potatoes, onions and pork chops done to a turn.

"There is scant rest on a way freight and before long the train, which flies the white flag which means no set schedule, is puffing along to the next stop. Slow as would seem the pace, there is never a dull moment. At Pine Orchard we drop off four of the gravel cars and shunt them over to be picked up at the convenience of a work train. Thus lightened of its load, the engine chugs more speedily back to recover the van and the remaining cars. For all this, I have a box seat as it were; a commanding view of the activities. The crew never tires when opportunity presents

Steam locomotive emerging from under CN bridge, Don Mills Road.

itself to explain to me the various signals, the delicate operation of meeting trains. Operating a railroad calls for endless meticulous synchronizing of individual effort. The men are well aware of their individual responsibilities. I became familiar with some of the terms and expressions which make up the argot of the railway men, of which "blowing the boiler" and "sitting in the hole" are typical.

"At Mount Albert there is an unexpected job yet one from which the way freight derives its name: the train sidles alongside of the freight shed and the brakeman and conductor heave to with a will. Washing machines, agricultural implements, soap, food, etc., in packages, large and small, are wheeled into the shed. Operations somewhat similar take place at Zephyr, Cedar Brae and Pefferlaw.

"At Beaverton the calm placid reach of Lake Simcoe breaks in on the scene. As the train hugs the shore of the lake, summer cottages dart by with the frequency of telegraph poles. But the lake and its necklace of cottages is only a facade for the real business of this countryside, which is easily seen at a glance in the stacked-up wheat, the buckwheat fields of buttermilk hue, herds of roaming cattle, indeed all of the attributes of an agricultural region showing itself off as a land of plenty.

"At Rathburn rock begins to show through the soil in quantity. The train ambles over the peagreen waters of the Couchiching River and we are in the railway yards of Washago. Beyond Washago rock strews the landscape in earnest. In a sense, the countryside has put on a shield; one dotted with lakes and studded with clumps of shaggy pine trees.

"At 10 o'clock in the evening the way freight, now reduced to engine and van, puffs into Gravenhurst, 112 miles and 14 hours from Toronto's Union Station: quite often the trip takes 16 hours. If you suggest that this is a long day, and it is, the men will reply with a shrug, 'That is railroading and there is nothing to be done about it.'

"The next morning the process of widening the distance between the engine and van and filling it with boxcars is commenced all over again. Interminable switching and sidetracking bring in empty cars to this caravan on rails, something like a rancher would cajole horses into a corral.

"The train branches off onto a side line into Sutton and which the crew call "the scenic railway". It is all of that. The way freight backs out again. From the platform of the van the rhythmic cadence of the wheel trucks striking the rail joints is heard. The scenery rises up to meet one while the thrilling, subtle scent of buckwheat mingled with moist woodlands permeates the air. Rarely have I enjoyed a ride as much.

"When every other morning comes around, and No. 1360 can be seen from my bedroom windows puffing around the end in a sweep of the Don Valley, I'll think beyond the hoarse hoot of the engine and its creaking, rasping cortege, or stiff-jointed boxcars, to the men who ride the way of the Bala way freight".

CHAPTER SIX

The Conservation Specials

By 1950 the Don Valley Conservation Association was in the throes of its campaign for the Conservation of the Don Valley. Everything that had been done up until then seemed to follow a familiar routine of printed folders, meetings, drives for membership, protests to various municipal groups, tree planting and, in some instances, concerts.

I felt that we needed something more sensational to attract public attention and focus it on the preservation of the greenbelt. Then I had an idea which struck me as unique and which would undoubtedly provide a stimulus for public attention: the D.V.C.A. would organize a steam locomotive trip and re-enact Governor Simcoe's exploit of September 1793 when he set out to explore the headwaters of the Don River in the vicinity of Richmond Hill.

The steam locomotive trip, which took place on Sunday, May 13, 1951, attracted 800 people. It succeeded far beyond our expectations. The presence of Governor Simcoe, Mrs. Simcoe, the aide-de-camp and his wife (the 1951 versions), added some pageantry and glamour to the event.

Our initial success prompted the D.V.C.A. to undertake further steam locomotive trips, some 11 in all. On one of these excursions, 1,000 participants were carried in 17 coaches, pulled by the largest passenger locomotive on the CNR. A brief description of some of these events follows in this chapter.

For generations the Don Station, now removed to the village of Todmorden Mills, was a familiar landmark in east Toronto. The station was built originally as part of the Belt Line Railway. In my day passengers could board trains departing for Montreal or Ottawa at the Don Station. In the tradition of the day, the station waiting room was equipped with a huge cast iron coal burning stove.

Much could be written about trains running over the tracks through the Don Valley. It was a busy line, serving the Toronto-Winnipeg passenger route, a local service to Beaverton and, during the summer, special trains to Muskoka.

A station house stood in the Valley at a junction of two lines about a quarter mile north of where the Leaside bridge is today. Passengers coming in from the West left the train at this station and walked across

East York High School students, impersonating Governor and Mrs. Simcoe (left) Aide de camp and wife, right, following Don Valley Conservation Association train trip to Richmond Hill May 1951. Photo taken at Fantasy Farm.

the platform to board a train leaving for Montreal. We referred to this line, which ran through Taylor's Bush ravine, as the Canadian Northern. The line was still operating for freight up until the mid-twenties. It was later abandoned and the rails removed. Today the right-of-way can scarcely be seen. Stretches of it lie in pools of surface water emerging from the numerous springs in the Taylor Creek Valley.

I am ever mindful of opportunities to take the "Northland" or the "Northlander", both excellent passenger trains which run over the Don Valley line. I see them frequently on their way in or out of the city.

Whenever I am seated in one of these trains I am filled with excitement as I watch the familiar Don Valley scenes flash by. The freshness and love for these scenes of my youth has never diminished.

These two trains are all that are left of the once busy schedule of steam locomotives that used the Don Valley line. However the Go trains have added a new dimension. I watch them go by, either from my patio or my bedroom window, both of which command a fine view of the Valley. Their schedule is so accurate that I can set my watch to the trains whistling the Pottery Road crossing.

The passengers who ride these trains are fortunate. They live in the suburbs and can leave their Richmond Hill homes and can travel quite at ease in a modern train with an added advantage of beautiful scen-

*ery en route. I hope the scenery means something to them. The Valley that
flashes by their windows was at one time a battleground where another
generation fought to preserve some of the wild and beautiful places of
our heritage. While I recognize that "progress" is inevitable in many
areas, it is comforting that our so-called golden years are so sprinkled
with golden memories.*

There appears in the front pages of *Remembering the Don* a double page
illustration of the Don Station at the Queen Street bridge. A crowd of people watch as a steam-powered locomotive pulls a long line of coaches into
the station. The date was May 18, 1952 and the train was bound for Mount
Albert, about 40 miles north of the city. Since then the Don Station has
been moved to Todmorden Mills, the steam-powered locomotives have
all but disappeared and it would be difficult to trace the whereabouts of
the 1,000 people who boarded the train for the excursion north. A year
before a similar excursion by train, sponsored by the D.V.C.A., departed
from the Don Station on May 13, 1951. It all happened this way.

Since boyhood days I have had a love for trains. Anyone who lived
anywhere over the Don bridge, from Eastern Avenue to Greenwood Avenue, as we did, knew all about trains. The main CNR line was just a few
blocks away and all day long and far into the night we could hear the
giants of steam huffing and puffing up the grade to Danforth Station at
Main Street. Several times an hour the street gates went down and people would witness the passenger and freight trains panting up the long
grade, or whizzing by on the down grade on the run in from Montreal
or Ottawa. Then there was the giant locomotive built especially to haul
freight up this grade. It was something to look at. In those days trains were
in my blood and they still are.

One day I was pondering how we could, in a spectacular way, focus
attention on the Don Valley Conservation Association and its campaign
to save the Don Valley, something that would also sell conservation to
the general public. Then it came to me in a flash: we could sponsor a train
trip and link it with an historical event. I had just finished reading the
Simcoe papers and knew that Governor Simcoe had set out on an expe-
dition of several days length to explore the headwaters of the Don. This
would have taken him to where Richmond Hill is today. My idea was to
take Governor and Mrs. Simcoe and the aide-de-camp and his wife on a
return trip to Richmond Hill via CNR. Everyone could dress up for the
occasion – and we did.

Hiring a train was an uncomplicated matter in those days. When we
planned the Richmond Hill trip the passenger agent, Ernie Brown,
attended the D.V.C.A. planning meeting. He required a guarantee of $300
to provide the train. A show of hands from the floor met the guarantee
and we were literally on our way then and there.

Re-enactment of Governor Simcoe's trip up the Don to Richmond Hill, 1951.

The ensuing trip was carried out in a blaze of glory. Our "Simcoe Special" carried 800 passengers plus a band of drummers and pipers. The group proceeded up the Valley, staged the planned historical pantomime in Richmond Hill and got full front page coverage in the *Globe and Mail* next morning.

From 1951 to 1961 we promoted 11 steam locomotive excursions, sometimes with a spring and fall trip in the same year. What was particularly gratifying about organizing these trips was that we brought people together who, for the most part, had never been on a train before. The itineraries of these trips included Mount Albert, Vandorf, Peterborough, Niagara Falls, Cobourg, Lindsay and Uxbridge. The destinations selected were within easy reach to keep down the cost of the tickets but also to allow time for a visit to a small centre and to provide for our conservation ceremonies, for such they were.

Every trip was staged around an event. When we went to Vandorf we featured Chief Big White Owl, who planted a maple tree at the station while the East York brass band paraded along the country roads to the step of familiar tunes.

On some trips we carried up to 1,000 passengers in as many as 17 coaches. With this array of passengers and equipment much excitement was brought to many a small town. In Uxbridge, a Texan who managed the Canadian plant of a Dallas firm went all out to ensure a suitable welcome. He marshalled the entire municipal services of the town to greet us on arrival. But behind the speeches, the pantomimes, the pipers and the drums and the conservation talk were people just havng a good time. Those trips undoubtedly accomplished a great deal for family life and established many family friendships that lasted throughout the years. Our last and probably best trip was to Lindsay, when 900 passengers were carried over a line of light rails that had never before carried a great giant of steam. The grade almost stopped the train in its tracks.

But on every trip the weather was the big, all important factor. There was usually an early rush for tickets but many people just sat back and waited to see what the weather would bring, as I did. As the great day approached it was sometimes preceeded by rain for several days, even up to the night before. I passed many a restless night wondering how things would work out. I should have had more confidence. The day was clear and the sun shone on every one of those trips. In all of those years we were never rained out once, although the Uxbridge outing was a rather chilly one.

The D.V.C.A. had a marvellous Train Committee. Herb Macauley handled ticket sales with expertise. The committee members ensured that everything took place as planned on the great day. There was not one unpleasant experience in 11 trips, or an looked-for event, excepting one. On the return trip from Lindsay the conductor of the train asked two passengers to change their plans and leave the train at Stouffville rather than Uxbridge. ''Because,'' said the conductor, ''if I stop this train at Uxbridge I will not get it back to Toronto today. There's too much grade. You saw what happened at Dixon's Hill!''

How does one assess the rewards of all of this effort? Well, there is something to be said about arriving at Union Station to see long lines of people thrilled with the prospect of boarding the waiting locomotive. The togged-up railway buffs crowd around the engine and the long line of coaches fades into the darkness of the station. One quickly becomes overwhelmed by it all.

By and by the train leaves the shelter of the station and starts its run up the long grade to Danforth Station. From there it passes into the open countryside of Scarborough, which it was in those days, and suddenly one is filled with a sense of wonder and excitement. The farm fences are lined with people who wave, and to whom one waves back, ducking cinders from the locomotive stack, while the cattle race across the fields. The train whistle has a particularly haunting beauty. The engineers were practiced in the art of pulling the whistle to draw from it the long, wailing, piercing shrieks that could tear the soul of a railway buff to shreds. There is simply nothing to compare with the sound of a blast from the whistle of a steam locomotive. It causes one to think of the thousands and thousands of times those war whoops of steam echoed from the forests or rocks of the north shore of Lake Superior and other wilderness areas across Canada.

Chief Big White Owl (Jasper Hill) and author plant a tree at Vandorf.

Finally the train arrives at its destination and the pent-up excitement of carrying out a program planned months before is released. Following the ceremony and its success one experiences the sudden euphoria of a job well done, along with the sudden disappearance of all strain. The hours pass quickly as we all engage in many animated, off the cuff conversations on our stroll through the town. All too soon we have to board the train for our return journey.

There is nothing to worry about now. As so many times before one finds a cozy corner in a coach, props oneself on an elbow and gazes out the window as the scenery goes speeding by to the cadence of clickity, clickity, clickity, click as the wheels strike the spaces between the rails with increasing speed. Many times I have listened to the wailing of the whistle while the cedar, balsam and spruce groves hurried by and wondered why I loved this scenery so much.

Then the next day the world knew what we had done when our conservation messages appeared in print, very often prominently displayed in the newspapers. Without the sustained effort of the D.V.C.A. and its train trips and other promotions the Valley, in my view, would not have been preserved as it is today. So it was worthwhile.

There are very few of the steam locomotives left. They all passed away so quickly – actually almost overnight. One day we had them, like an old friend, but the next day they were gone, hurried off the scene with their smoke and their ashes as quickly as possible. But what remained was the love that tens of thousands of people had for the steam locomotive, a love which lasted lifetimes. I recall with sadness the scene of perhaps a hundred steam locomotives, rusted and idle, awaiting their fate in the furnaces of steel mills, lined up on the tracks at Allandale, now a part of Barrie. Weeks later they were gone. A few were saved at Barrie, Guelph, Toronto and Niagara Falls and placed close to railway stations in mute testimony to their role in bygone days. They were big attractions for the people who crowded the platform of the Don Valley Station or filled the concourse of the Union Station to proclaim to the world that they were conservation-minded and likewise steam-locomotive-minded. We never could separate one from the other. In my mind the "Conservation Specials" live on and on.

The Don Station had a colourful history, having been built originally to serve as a stop on the Belt Line Railway. People of a later generation wondered why the station was tucked out of the way in the shadow of the Queen Street bridge and why it was so close to Union Station. But the present Queen Street bridge was not there in the 1880s when the station was built. An earlier bridge was on a level with the crossing, which of course put the station in a normal position. As for its location, the station, built long before the days of rapid transportation, was a fair distance from Union Station.

But then one day came the news that the Don Station was to be demolished as there was no further use for it. It so happened about this time that I attended a meeting of the Todmorden Mills committee. Someone pointed to the need for extra storage space in the village. "Why," I inquired, "don't you try to get the old Don Station?" Bert Pratt, who sat on the committee, recorded this suggestion. Action was taken and no doubt True Davidson had a hand in it.

It was found that the station could be moved and in due course it was cut into two pieces and conveyed to its present site at Todmorden Mills. A railroader who had read about the station's plight in the newspapers provided the required sum of $7,000 to have the station moved. It is a pity that the hero who contributed the funds has remained unnamed and unsung.

I was personally pleased that the station had been saved because it was a place of special memories. Our family lived on Munro Street when the Don Station was still being used. The present Queen Street bridge had been built at the time and as a child, I walked over that bridge to school with my brothers and sisters. It provided good views of the rail traffic below. But one event among these childhood memories remains ever present. It was on a Saturday afternoon in the early fall of 1914, as I recall it, when we went to the bridge to see the soldiers. There they were on the station platform, hundreds and hundreds of them in their kilts with rifles, kit bags and dunnage, with the coaches drawn up alongside the platform. As I learned later, these soldiers were the 48th Battalion High-

View of Don Station, as moved to Todmorden Village.

landers en route to the East Coast and eventually France. Ahead of them lay the railway to Leaside, the open countryside of Eastern Ontario and four years of an unforgettable war.

This incident was confirmed in *48th Highlanders of Canada* written by Kim Beattie and pubished in 1932. This extract is from page 20.

> *"Every man thrilled to his sole-studs as the pipers came in with "London Bridge", and the Highlanders (15th Battalion C.E.F.) swung out of the Armouries (University Avenue) into the rain, to move down streets jammed with people in a fever of excitement throughout their march to the Don Station. Easily 100,000 people were assembled in the downpour; they overflowed the Don River bridge and nearby streets to wish godspeed to the Highlanders who were off to war. The train pulled out on time and the cheers of Toronto grew dim as they rolled eastwards.... The parade strength as the battalion headed eastwards for Valcartier was 970 all ranks. The day was August 29th, 1914"*

For the next four years the Don station was a mute witness to countless departures and arrivals and soldiers as the war dragged on, many of them in more tragic circumstances than the gala atmosphere of the first departure of troops as related above.

Charles Sauriol with engineer on CN train excursion up the Don, 1961.

Today the station, like a gentle old lady in a cozy kitchen, stands ensconced in the trees of Todmorden Mills, as tranquil as the atmosphere of a hot July afternoon.

It seems appropriate at this point to make additional references to trains of the Don Valley. There were numerous train accidents. The first I heard of occurred in 1910 or thereabouts when the track had been first laid up the Valley. It is a story which has been passed on to me.

It was in the spring of the year and during a warm day water had flowed abundantly down a railway embankment and poured over the rails. With nightfall, however, the water covering the rails had frozen solid. Along came the shunting engine and when the wheels struck the ice, the train simply spun off the rails. The locomotive toppled over and the engineer and fireman were both killed. This occurred at a point across the river from MacLean's sugar bush.

There were several other train derailments, recorded as follows: on March 21, 1949, 40 cars loaded with new trucks were derailed near the Winchester Street cross due to a soft roadbed, caused, no doubt, by spring thaws. The newspapers of the day carried illustrated articles of the accident. However the derailment that really stands out was on December 2, 1949. I have some excellent photocopies of the reports of this event, taken from newspapers of the time. This accident occurred within view of Lawrence Avenue, where it now crosses the Valley. At about 7:30 a.m. a freight train was puffing up the Valley when it unexpectedly collided

All aboard for the Conservation Special, Don station circa 1954.

with the Winnipeg passenger train travelling in the opposite direction. The locomotives crashed head on. There was no loss of life, although extensive damage to rolling stock resulted from the collision.

There have been instances where trains have gone off the rails during a heavy rain, or where they travelled very slowly after a flood. In the old days the Don Valley Flats, including the railway tracks, were often under water.

We were not supposed to trespass on the line but we did. It was the best way to walk up the East Valley. This was always hazardous because of the trestles. If a train came along when you were in the middle of one it could be dangerous so we were always very careful. There were pranksters in my day and some of their pranks were not funny. For example, they would throw new ties into the river or pile some of them on the rails, hoping that a train would strike them. It was rather ghoulish and I removed them when I found them and alerted the railway police.

I was walking up the Valley one evening for a swim in Clay Banks swimming hole and had a long clear view ahead. Two young lads were walking toward me, deep in conversation. Suddenly a runaway boxcar rounded a distant bend. The lads seemed to be unaware of it. I waved my arms and shouted and they cleared the track in time. A few moments later a shunting engine rounded the bend at a fast clip in pursuit of the boxcar, which was recovered in Riverdale Park.

CHAPTER SEVEN

The Gray Family

Remembering the Don *did not include detailed mention of the Gray family. It is appropriate to devote a chapter of this book to this pioneer family, which is closely linked with the development of the East Don Valley.*

The *History of the County of York* includes references to the Gray family, which has long been identified with the history of the Don Valley. William Gray, who was born in Renfrewshire, Scotland in 1802, came to Canada with several of his brothers and settled in York. He built a grist mill on the East Don River "with two run of stones", meaning that the mill was equipped with two mill stones. His brother Alexander built a saw mill across the stream from the grist mill.

John Brooks of Toronto, who attended one of my lectures and is an historian of the Gray family in his own right, provided me with notes of a family history from which the following facts were taken.

The Gray family was Huguenot (French Protestant) in origin. William Gray's ancestors left France for Scotland during the persecution of the Huguenots in the reign of Louis XIV. They settled on a coastal island, moving later to Paisley. Their home in Paisley was near the site of a factory built at a later date for the Coats Thread company.

Alexander, who as a teenager lived with his grandfather, also named Alexander, wrote in his diary, "that in 1815, following the battle of Waterloo, veterans of the British army were encouraged to emigrate to Canada where they were assured of large grants of land." At some point between 1820 and 1823 Alexander and several of his brothers came to Canada, accompanied by their mother.

It took 16 weeks to cross the Atlantic. During this long voyage the vessel was buffeted by winds and drifted back and forth. But eventually the coast of Canada was reached and the family made its way in stages to what is now Kingston, en route westward to York.

The Don Valley was at that time being alloted to settlers and the Gray family settled on lot 9, concession, 3, York. It was very much a wilderness area in those days. The family's grants were such that they eventually owned a 960-acre tract along the Don.

A member of the pioneer Gray family named Harold, son of Timothy Gray, wrote in his diary, "To the best of my knowledge my grandfather
William built the grist mill. His house and a second one for his miller were
built beside the mill."

William, Alexander and James Gray worked together to build their
homes and fortunes along the Don. Alexander's saw mill was directly
across the river from Alexander's grist mill. they were in the habit of calling across the Don to each other when either one or the other wanted
a greater surge of power. This meant opening the sluice to provide more
water from the mill race.

James, of whom we know little, located up the Valley slope above
William. Two other brothers, John and George, also homesteaded along
the Don. John settled on property east of Alexander.

On June 8, 1947 I met George Gray, who resided at the time at 78
Ellerbeck Avenue near Danforth and Broadview. He told me sadly that
he was the last of the Grays. He was born on August 15, 1863 and was 84
years of age when I met him in 1947. His father, William Gray, was born
in 1802. William Gray was 61 years of age when George, the last of 13
children, was born. It seems incredible that a man who walked on Danforth Avenue in 1947 had a father born thirteen years before the battle
of Waterloo, but it's true.

George Gray also told me that his uncle James came to Canada as a
soldier in the British army. He was four months on the water. When his
regiment arrived in Canada the War of 1812 was over. James settled in
Canada and operated a distillery near his brothers' grist and saw mills.

The Gray dam on which the mills depended for water was strong
enough to withstand river pressure in all seasons. It had to be strong to
survive the impact of ice floes which followed the spring break-up of river
ice. The side walls of the dam were constructed so the river current would
not side-cut the dam. The mills were built with wood from trees cut in
the Valley. White pine served for framework, bins and general use. Hard
maple was used to make gears, shafts and the water wheels.

The site on which the Gray mills stood was bought in 1915 by Mr.
Moffatt Dunlop and the property became known as Don-Alda Farm. This
is how I first knew it. The property in my time was reputed to be one of
the finest landscaped rural holdings in Ontario. In 1949 I described it this
way:

*"Farm lands and woodlands reach from the Don Mills Road
to the extension of Woodbine Avenue on the east. The main
farm buildings are clustered on the site of the Gray mill. The
Don-Alda herd of Jersey cattle is an outstanding feature of the
countryside. A stretch of ravine and woodland is adjacent to
Don-Alda on the east."*

Today the Don-Alda stretch of the East Don Valley, bounded on the north by York Mills Road, has been beautifully preserved in the tradition of the original Don-Alda Farm. It is still landscaped beautifully, although no longer ensconced in woodlands. These have been replaced by housing, hotels and office buildings. Of the presence of the Grays, there remains not a trace.

CHAPTER EIGHT

Ashes and Embers

A dream that I cherished at one time in my life was to write a story of the outdoors with a particular appeal to boys, a book that would express my feelings for the preservation of the ravines and valleys of southern Ontario. The end result of this dream was "Ashes and Embers", the story of a young scout whose outdoor camping and hiking experiences were for the most part mine. The title, "Ashes and Embers", was the symbol of the camp fire. There was the added drama of the discovery on the hero's part of a secret dyeing formula in the old (Milne) mill. It was written during the period of January to December 1945, was suitably illustrated and when completed was a rather good effort, or so I thought.

The story I felt would soon become popular with boys, for it was about the things outdoor-minded boys want to read. Full of confidence I approached certain Authorities for endorsement and support. But I must have been corresponding with a lackey, judging from his inconsiderate and negative response. He seemed anxious to remove me and my book from his life post-haste.

Any author has stories of disappointment and perhaps I should have pursued my attempts to have the story published. But there were other matters requiring attention, so "Ashes and Embers" was relegated to my library shelf, where it has remained to this day.

However recently I leafed through its pages and was struck with the quality of its predictions. As a person who has made a career of conservation, and been one of the major contributors in this field in Canada, "Ashes and Embers" appeals to me in retrospect as a worthy effort.

The hero of the story, whose name is Don, sets out to save Pine Valley – and does. He proposes planning and conservation measures that are decades before their time, long before anyone had heard of conservation authorities, greenbelt or other phrases connected with the preservation of natural values as we know them today. In this, "Ashes and Embers" was prophetic. Actually it amazes me, as one who had a major hand in implementing the Toronto greenbelt plan, just how prophetic the story was.

Now, some 40 years after the story was written, I plan to rewrite it, not as a boy's book, but drawing comparisons with its message and the ethics of today. The sketches, done by a young lad, while the work of an amateur, have a unique quality about them that should be preserved.

During the thirties I set my mind to the task of writing a book for boys. It was late 1945 before I actually finished the manuscript, the story of a small boy and his adventures in Pine Valley. The plot of the story was centered on a secret dyeing formula discovered by our hero in an old woollen mill in Pine Valley. It was rather a good story and has weathered the harsh light of rereadings, when one is inclined to be critical of one's earlier efforts.

It is significant that the ideas I expressed in that story were well ahead of their time, when "preservation of the environment", "conservation" and "reforestation" were only words in the dictionary. The inception of the conservation authority movement occurred in 1946, well after my story opted for the preservation of an entire valley, Pine Valley was of course the Don Valley and the general mosaic of the story is made up largely of my boyhood experiences there.

In 1950 I took my manuscript, "History of the Don Valley", on which I had worked for 20 years, to one of the most prominent book publishers of the time. The man who assessed manuscripts said, "No one will ever read this. Who is interested in the Don Valley?" I kept on with my work and my writing. I produced *The Cardinal* and ran choice extracts from my history there. Selected issues of *The Cardinal* were eventually gathered together and published as *Remembering the Don*, whose success has been outstanding. There is no doubt that the interest in our recent history is much more intense today than was true 30 or more years ago.

While writing these *Tales of the Don* I again leafed through the long-neglected manuscript of "Ashes and Embers". The prophetic quality of the last chapter struck me. It was as though I had been able to look into a crystal ball and see future events. I felt that part of that chapter should be reproduced. At the time, in 1945, it was pure fantasy, wishful dreaming. In 1957 I became chairman of the Conservation Areas Advisory Board of the Metropolitan Region Conservation Authority. I had an initial yearly budget of $500,000 for the purchase of natural area land, or ten times the imaginary figure that was mentioned in my writing in 1945. It is all very stimulating for me at this date to think of myself as one of the few men whose dreams, so many bubbles in the air when they first sprang to mind, became realities.

Our hero in "Ashes and Embers" was one of those individuals born with a bit of a willow branch in his mouth, rather than the traditional silver spoon. He was one of those persons who so inherently love nature that they want to save whatever beauty comes across their path. So our hero, Don, sets out to save Pine Valley. To quote from "Ashes and Embers":

"Finally the Scoutmaster said, 'The letter I received a few days ago outlines a plan for the preservation of the valley as defined by the local council which has taken steps to preserve the valley along a length of twelve miles. Henceforth it will be classed as greenbelt and will be subject to a rigid control of its woodlands and wildlife. The program is as follows:

An annual budget of $50,00 (subject to yearly increase) for maintaining the woodlands. This will consist of:
– Patrolling the valley to eliminate all misuse of the woods whatsoever.
– There will be an annual tree planting of 50,000 seedling trees through scouts and school groups.
– Bird life will be protected and likewise wild flower colonies and particularly the trillium.
– Educational exhibits will be placed at entry points to indoctrinate people in the use of the woodlands.
– The streams are to be restocked with fish.
– Outdoor camping sites will be established for the use of Scouts, hiking groups and other responsible parties.
– A central lodge will be built under the control of the Little Fort Naturalist Society for the purposes of conducting nature classes for interested persons. The lodge will be maintained for the use of skiers during the winter months.
– Several slopes will be cleared for trails for cross-country skiing.'

'Why Eric that's astounding progress. Who would have ever thought of all that. The council claims that it got most of these ideas from listening to you talk, and unanimously approved their adoption. Well they didn't leave anything out, did they. No they didn't for there is still another item, to identify and mark all original mill sites and other places of historical interest.'"

Today there is a generation of naturalists, biologists, environmentalists and conservationists who are identified with outdoor education centres. The programs there are directed to education in conservation, following the concept that "Ashes and Embers" foresaw 40 years ago. Likewise thousands of people today are either employed or otherwise associated with conservation authorities or metropolitan regional park systems. Here again is a concept foreseen in "Ashes and Embers". Today the historical aspects of our culture are held in high regard, not only by a society or two dedicated to this work but in dozens of ways visible through the preservation of pioneer villages, individual dwellings and artifacts. Great sums of money are being spent today to preserve valley systems and wetlands and for the survival of habitat bird and animal species. As for cross-country skiing, also foretold in "Ashes and Embers", it has grown from a few individuals stomping through the woods on old-fashioned skis to a very popular recreational pursuit.

All of this was foreseen in "Ashes and Embers", which makes the text unusual. In the '30s and '40s I was indeed a voice preaching in the wilderness and my book was met with indifference and misunderstanding. But today the fruits of my forethought, and those of the people who inspired it, are very evident. "Ashes and Embers", though it remains a single copy lost on a bookshelf, spawned ideas that went farther afield and found expression in other ways. I like to think of it as a feeble candle that lighted the way to the end of the tunnel. One of our politicians of the late forties, talking about the conservation movement, exclaimed one day, and the clipping is still in my files, "There is nothing to this but a few bird watchers running around with binoculars." This proved to be an understatement of gigantic proportions considering the millions of people who today use the Toronto greenbelt for recreational and outdoor education purposes.

CHAPTER NINE

Playing along the Don

Cycling, hiking, canoeing and skating are practised today to an extent that would have overwhelmed the imagination and means of the boys of my day. Having said this, I do not choose to prove that in the '20s we were smarter, tougher and more outdoors-minded than boys of today, because this was not so.

We had to make do with what we had and there was little money to do it with. I recall how excited we boys were one camping trip up the Don when one of the fellows, who had a homemade receiving set, picked up a signal from Toronto Island. Imagine, all the way from the Island, six or seven miles from the old swimming hole.

But in our way we had fun and the Don Valley contributed largely to it. In some measure we are spoiled today. While it is possible to use the same facilities as in my day, they seem drab compared to the wilderness areas that beckon from far afield. The next chapter is my salute to the biking, hiking, canoeing and skating days up the Don, as we knew them.

Cycling was the all-important sport for the boys of my generation. We all had bikes to get around in and out of the city. Furthermore there were relatively few motor cars to compete with. By the late '20s my $12 "boneshaker" had been replaced by a beautifully made, semi-racing model "Planet" bicycle that cost $60 new. For night riding it was equipped with a carbide light. Carbide pellets were placed in the can of the lamp where they generated a gas which, when ignited, projected a clear white light a hundred feet or more ahead of the bike. Biking started just as soon as snow left the ground and stopped when the ground was again snow-covered.

In those days there was little housing north of Danforth Avenue. We lived on Leslie Street at Gerrard at the time. I have recollections of cycling along the coke walkway that flanked Donlands Avenue from Mortimer to Don Mills Road and of the tremendous old red oak tree that stood on the east side of Donlands, just south of Don Mills Road. Donlands was often a mud patch so we biked while we could along the coke walkway. The stretch east of Pape on what was then Don Mills Road, now O'Connor Drive, was all fields.

One of my favourite runs in my heyday as a cyclist was to Agincourt and back, a distance of some 24 miles. I did this either on weekends or on Friday evenings. We took everything for granted in those days and felt that the scenes with which we were familiar would never change. I often cycled to Agincourt without seeing more than an occasional motor car. From the top of de Grassi Hill it was all open country. I got to know every tree, woodlot and dwelling on the 12 mile stretch. How quaint and rural it would seem today. There was the Meagher homestead near the edge of the Valley, then the fine and stately Taylor pioneer homestead where the Science Centre now stands. Beyond this the Canadian Pacific line crossed the road. There was a pump on the east side of Don Mills Road, just south of the railway at the entrance to Donlands Farm. It was customary for me to stop there for a drink, at what is today one of the busiest intersections in Canada.

Immediately to the north of the railway stood a fringe of woodland on the west and a woodlot on the east. There were three dwellings between the railway and Lawrence Avenue. Today all of this land is covered with factories or housing. Watson's was the landmark at Lawrence and Don Mills and across from it was the Don School, built in 1853. Then at York Mills stood the Muirhead pioneer home. Here the road wound eastwards into the Valley where the river was spanned by a cement bridge, with Don-Alda Farm to the south. From here on to Agincourt it was open fields, with the occasional dwelling.

Agincourt, then a hamlet, was the high-tide of the tour. It was down grade all the way back, easy pedalling along Kennedy Road to Danforth, along Danforth and down the grade of Gerrard Street home. Incredibly all this has changed beyond recognition within a scant 50 or 60 years.

At times there were variations to the Agincourt trip when I cycled westward to the remote hamlet of Oriole, which I sometimes referred to as "Saur-iole". This area, I learned from studying old maps, had been glebe land. At Oriole, where there was a pumping station, lands to the north fringed on the woodlands of German Creek, at that time very much in the open countryside. The road along which I pedalled from Don Mills Road to Oriole bore the unfamiliar name of Sheppard Avenue.

Duncan was another hamlet I visited. There was a church at what is now the northwest corner of Lawrence Avenue and Leslie. Duncan had once been a stop on the Canadian National line. However for me Duncan was a place to stop for a rest when I walked up Wilket Creek ravine, about where Edwards Gardens now stands. From there, after the rest at Duncan, I walked along country roads to the East Valley of the Don. There was another stop at the Milne Mill and thence down Valley to my cottage again. Milne Mill stood in what was known as Milne Hollow.

Cycling was supplemented by my personal craze for walking. The Don Valley was quite unspoiled and a person could walk there for hours without any human interruption. I have often travelled by car to what is now York Mills and the Don Valley Parkway, all fields and woods 50 years ago. From here I would walk back to my cottage, following the ravine system and taking most of the day to complete the trip, either in summer or winter. The calculated stops were the Milne Woollen Mill, which was later demolished but which should have been left, and the MacLean's sugar bush and shanty. The next stop was the Clay Banks swimming hole where on a hot day I would stop for a swim. From there I walked back to the Forks of the Don.

There has always been canoeing on the Don since the day that the Jesuit priest, Father Pierre Raffeix, first mapped the Don River in 1688. For several years an annual canoe trip down the Don was held in which hundreds of canoeists participated. Then there have been isolated cases of individuals braving the shallow, small rapids and other obstacles to canoe down the Don. However, Roy Cadwell, a founder of the Don Valley Conservation Association, masterminded the D.V.C.A.'s first canoe trip. It took place on May 24, 1948, starting from the very narrow part of the Don at Thornhill and working downstream. I took all day to reach RIVERDALE PARK.

The Don Valley Hiking Club, an arm, or rather more to the point a leg, of the D.V.C.A. was a group of 30 to 40 people who perpetuated the traditions of the Don Valley Nature Study Club of 1900 (see *Remembering the Don*, pp 113-115). The Hiking Club tramped through areas far beyond the Don Valley, including the rolling moraine of Glen Major and to the north many miles beyond Uxbridge. These areas were reached, in some instances, by steam locomotive. For example, a group of us sometimes boarded the CPR steam locomotive for Montreal at Leaside Station. Leaving the train at Dagmar, a small way station, we walked ten miles along the roads to Uxbridge, stopping to make tea in the woods en route. We then took the Lindsay steam locomotive back to Toronto. This trip took a full day.

Another of our innovations was to motor to Uxbridge, leave the cars there, then take taxis to a point ten miles beyond and walk back along the wetlands system and railway to the cars.

Today the Outing Club of East York also ranges the Don Valley on planned hikes, at times taking public transportation to a distant point then walking back along the ravine system.

The river ice was indeed a boy's paradise. In the '20s and '30s, and probably before, boys used the Don for winter sport whenever it could be used. Skating along the river for miles was a popular pastime. It was a joy to whizz along, following the turns of the evergreen-draped river banks all the way up to Lawrence Avenue and farther. Ideal skating conditions were present in March but not just along the Don. At times a combination of melted snow and rain turned farm fields into ponds, which stood frozen when the temperature dropped. I have seen these sheets of

One of the many Don swimming holes. This one up CN track a quarter mile from Don Mills Road, 1935.

ice alongside Don Mills Road where the Science Centre now stands. They were the best skating rinks ever.

Skating along the Don persisted until the 1950s. There were all kinds of places over which to skate. First there were long stretches of clean ice on the river. Then there were the frog ponds. These were usually water-filled channels of the former course of the Don, before it was straightened either by man or nature. Groups of boys would spend a day at a time, playing shinny on the ice. There was always a large bonfire built as there was always a supply of deadwood around. Then there were the quarries, but they were dangerous because the ice often gave way and drownings resulted. The same was true of the old mill dams on the Don, several of which were blown up in my time because of accidents that happened there. Anyone who frequented the Don in winter could usually say that he had fallen in at some time or another.

INTRODUCTION TO PART TWO

The stories which follow in Part Two of *Tales of the Don* stem from my personal activities in the Don Valley from the 1930s to the 1960s.

A few observations about storytelling are in order: there are several ways to write a story. One is to construct it with phrases that flow from a master's pen. Another way is to write the story as one would tell it to a friend by a fireside. "Gee, that's the way Charlie talks." Or it could be Dad or Eric or whoever. Thus the stamp of one's writing is as individual as a signature, and perhaps it is the best way of writing.

My second observation, perhaps trite, is that life is made up of commonplace, everyday events that often have a humorous twist, although we may not have thought so at the time. There is something rewarding about telling or writing a story which, like an old snapshot, recalls an event long past. When the story is told, the harshness or inconvenience suffered at the time has been dissolved by time and only the essence of the memory remains.

There is nothing sensational or dramatic about my memories of the Don but they have stood the test of time. They are good stories to my mind, full of such good memories. They are also good friends, ever faithful.

CHAPTER TEN

Maple Sap and Syrup

Making maple syrup was only one of the joys available to me living at the Forks of the Don. The trees were there, practically at my doorstep, and all I had to do was take the time to learn how to gather the sap and boil it down to get some of the elixir of spring, for that's what maple syrup is.

It is very apt that the first story begins with spring, the time of year when the harshness of winter gives way like the snow before the warming sun to a new cycle of life. Spring is announced by the caw of the crow, the hooded spathe of the skunk cabbage pushing through the icy snow and the tinkling of maple sap in a pail.

This chapter had been written when I came across some interesting items about W.F. (Billy) MacLean while leafing through copies of the Toronto World *of 1907 at the* Toronto Reference Library. *These items were added to the chapter.*

It is reasonably safe to say that the combination of hard maple trees, the woods in March and running sap has gripped the imagination of Eastern Canada's inhabitants since sap first poured from maple trees chipped with an axe to fall into birch back receptacles.

From my earliest outdoor days I saw the maple sugar shanty and its accoutrements as the symbols of spring. Here at long last was evidence that spring was preparing to push winter away. Soon the burgeoning foliage and pastel tints of the first woodland wild flowers would cover the Valley.

While I was deeply imbued with the romance of syrup making, I had never even tapped a tree until I first hiked up the East Valley of the Don in 1920 with scouts of the 45th troop. Even then all we did on our spring outings was scrape a few holes in the maple bark to get a sip of the sap as it poured out over the tree trunk.

However when I acquired my acreage on the Don, gathering maple sap did indeed become a reality. In those days Meredith Hardware on King Street East, near Jarvis, sold sap spouts, pails and whatever else a person needed to make syrup. I soon had a modest supply of all the necessary equipment.

The making of maple syrup in the Don Valley and MacLean's sugar bush are synonymous. As a career conservationist I have seen many stands of hard maple over the past 40 years but none finer than the ancient hard maple trees that graced the slopes behind MacLean's shanty. They formed a grove between the Valley slopes and the river. There are still a few survivors to verify the truth of what I have said but in my day the maples were one of the natural features of the Don Valley. This brings me to my own particular adventures in making maple syrup.

In my youth, the receding snows of March brought maple syrup produced by the back country farmers to our table. My wife's father, who hailed from the Eastern Townships in Quebec, used to send us a gallon or so of the finest Quebec syrup. It was typical in those days for street vendors to pass along the streets of Montreal shouting their wares, with wagons sometimes loaded with more syrup than a man could be expected to produce. My father-in-law knew something about syrup. He would buy only after he had "hefted a gallon". If it was overly heavy he wouldn't buy, but if the syrup was light in weight he did. I doubt if a similar experience would be possible today, due to the high standards of maple syrup products bottled or canned under well-known brand labels in Quebec and elsewhere.

Some of the farm folk used to make syrup by whittling maple branches and boiling them in water. Add some mapleine or comparable product and you have a syrup of a kind. Something akin to this is sold in the stores today but identified on the label as such. I am also told that maple syrup can be made out of potato peelings but I never got around to trying my hand at it.

My first attempts at syrup making were confined to a few soft maple trees near my property. The trees were selected, appropriate holes bored with an auger, apple juice cans were suspended from hooks and lo and behold, the magic water began to drop. Soon the cans were full. I look back at that sort of thing as among my happiest memories of the past. There was a lot more to it than making a few ounces of maple syrup. The sweet water was tasty on a sharp April evening. It tasted of spring and the woods and was a complete change from the city I had left a few minutes before.

With the passing years several changes took place in my life at the Forks of the Don. The property began to settle down into a pattern of a well-planned country holding, although still on the rustic side. When the family moved back to the city at the end of the summer, life at the cottage changed. There were perhaps seven of my friends who could be termed kindred souls who made a point of coming to the cottage every Saturday afternoon. They helped me immeasurably with all kinds of chores like collecting driftwood and making maple syrup. One of these men came from the north and what he didn't know about splitting and sawing wood and making maple syrup could be written off. With this

Saturday afternoon gang engaged in tree tapping.

kind of help I began to make syrup in earnest.

Over the years I tapped more and more trees, including some I had planted. By then I was boiling down the sap over an open fire fed with driftwood collected from the shores of the Don. One evening, as the sap was beginning to take on the aroma of a plausible syrup, I decided to finish the boiling down in the cottage. I was with Eric la Trobe at the time and before I retired for the night I set the five-gallon boiler full of syrupy water on the stove. The stove was an old-fashioned one which could hold huge chunks of wood about two feet long. It would heat a four room cottage very easily and quickly. Having loaded the stove with wood and closed the damper, I went to bed. While I slumbered peacefully the water in the boiler continued to steam, filling the cottage with the pleasing odour of maple syrup. It did something else too! When I awakened and came down to the living room to check the syrup, I found that all of the wallpaper within a few yards of the stove had been steamed off the walls. It was quite an experience.

I started by buying an evaporator from a Quebec foundry. Actually what I bought was a 60-gallon pan that sat over a stove bottom made to fit. The pan was supposed to be used for finishing off syrup only but I decided to use it for the full process. When a fire was lit under the pan, 60 gallons of water would begin to steam in minutes. It produced a terrific heat. I set up this outfit in my workshop and connected the stove to a chimney.

80

The best woods were to the east of my property in a curve in the Don where there were many large sugar maples. These were tapped and each evening several men came out to give me a hand bringing in the sap. I seem to have a propensity in life for doing things the hard way and this was one of them. The sap was poured into five-gallon drums and these had to be carried up a rather steep valley wall and conveyed to the workshop. Frost settles quickly on a late March or early April evening and the soft soil of mid-afternoon soon becomes as hard as a board and slippery too. All this compounded the problem of bringing in the maple water. However we did rather well and made several gallons of excellent syrup simply because we felt it was worth the effort.

One year the season was coming to an end and we were on the last batch. All during that week we had boiled and the water had steamed and the syrup had gradually thickened. We were on the last lap. It was Good Friday and a truly beautiful early April day, one of those soul-soothing days when spring breaks from its cocoon and it feels so good to be able to share the wonderful hours.

I planned to attend the Good Friday service and left my post for several hours to do so. I stoked the fire below the evaporator, swung the workshop doors open, very carefully adjusted the damper and left. Now during my days up the Don dozens of fellows made a habit of stopping by the cottage and saying hello. I can only surmise that one of these hikers or bird watchers had stepped into the workshop and, probably deciding that the wood fire was getting low, stoked it up again on my behalf. When making maple syrup, it's the final few minutes that count. The syrup may boil for hours but at a certain critical time the syrup will boil frantically. That is the precise time to get it away from the fire. Alas, I was not there at that precise time. When I arrived back about 4 o'clock all I saw, with unbelieving eyes, was a heavy, blackened crust of burnt sugar that had been my maple syrup. I could only think of something my father used to say, "So and so means well, but he grabs the wrong end."

The magic of maple syrup making still draws me like a magnet and awakens my memories of the past. The curling smoke from the sugar shanty, particularly those of the Muskoka district, are an ode to the birth of a new season. Likewise the more sophisticated efforts that the Conservation Authorities and the Ministry of Natural Resources have included in their educational programs.

I occasionally take a hike up the East Valley to where MacLean's sugar bush and its magnificent groves of ancient maple trees once stood. The sugar shanty is gone, the sap pails rusted away and only a few giant trees have been spared in the wake of local development. It all seems so long ago. The endless hikes to the sugar bush, the friends who shared them and the syrup that on that Good Friday burned to a crisp – are experiences I shall treasure.

Charles Sauriol pouring sap into container from trees near his cottage. March, mid '40's.

A FOOTNOTE TO W.F. MacLEAN

Mr. W.F. (Billy) MacLean, editor of the *Toronto World*, was very much a part of his maple syrup operation in the Don Valley. His publication was used on several occasions to market his products in addition to his political opinions. For example, there appeared in the *Toronto World* of March 23, 1907 a large advertisement which read as follows:

> "PURE MAPLE SYRUP AND SUGAR
> *Made at Donlands Farm, seven miles from Toronto's City Hall.*
> *Just maple sap evaporated down to syrup and sugar. Clean tin*
> *utensils from start to finish. We will have a hundred quarts*
> *made yesterday on sale at Michie and Co.'s 7 King Street West*
> *store. Today, Saturday, at 9:00 a.m. Guaranteed absolutely*
> *pure and clean. Fifty cents a quart bottle. Sugar in half-pound*
> *cakes."*

The name Michie's will evoke a few memories for older folk. Michie's was the gourmets' mecca at the time, specializing in exclusive food products. The store catered to an elite and very distinguished Toronto clientele.

In the March 29, 1907 issue of *Toronto World* there was a cartoon showing a man carrying two buckets of maple sap, with trees and a sugar shanty in the background. The bearded man in the drawing, Jack Canuck, is carrying the pails and talking to Uncle Sam, who is seated on a log. He is saying, "Well, Sam, if you and your English friend are over here to watch me make sugar, I'm glad to see you. If you are here to talk reciprocity, I'm too busy with important things." The inference is quite clear to anyone who recalls the days of Sir Wilfrid Laurier's fight for reciprocity with the United States.

CHAPTER ELEVEN

Hens and Eggs

My father, for whom I had unbounded respect, was a strong, heavily-built man who came to Toronto to dredge the Don, ostensibly for the purpose of bringing Lake Simcoe water to Toronto for drinking purposes. (See Remembering the Don, *pp 121-126.)*

There were seven children in our family, of which I was the youngest. Father never received a pension. He seldom, if ever, took holidays and then only in his declining years, with me, and worked until the month before he died at an advanced age. No one retired in those days. Two of his sons served in the Canadian Army during the first World War.

Father showed a tremendous interest in the acquisition of property at the Forks of the Don. Even though he always had a low income, he was able to acquire four houses. It seemed to him an opportunity to put a few latent dreams into action, one of which was raising poultry on a large scale to make a few dollars to tide him over.

As the story which follows shows, father was bent on raising poultry at the Forks of the Don. In the '20s and much later, keeping poultry was the thing to do in almost any backyard. We also kept ducks, which on a Sunday morning quacked enough to wake the neighbourhood. Father knew something about chickens and for many years our eggs came from the city coops, a stone's throw from the kitchen.

Jock (and this was not his name) looked like the man to get things going for Father. But as events proved, he was not. I do not say that he was dishonest, that would be an oversimplification. More to the truth was that he was desperate, and with so little to live on he may have done things that ordinarily he would not have done.

My regret now is that my father, like so many men of a few generations ago, had to work so hard for so little. Do we today really appreciate their efforts to ensure for us the lifestyle we enjoy? Had there been a Canada Pension Plan, Old Age Security or OHIP at the time, there would have been no need for Father, or men like him, to think about raising chickens for the few dollars they might provide.

Had I said to him, "Pa," (We always called him Pa, Dad came with a later generation.) "Pa, you are going to get about $500 a month now and it will increase as prices go up", he would have looked at me and said, "Son, I don't believe it. The world is going crazy."

*My story is amusing some 50 years after the event but there is pathos
in it when I reflect on the hardness of the times and the frailties of human
nature. It happened this way.*

We were at the high tide of the Depression when, on stepping out from
my cottage one midsummer Sunday morning, I saw that a tent had been
erected on a strip of land adjacent to the railway across the river from my
holdings. I discovered the facts later. An east Toronto tradesman, whom
we shall call Jock, his wife and apparently infirm daughter had packed
a few belongings and simply left their immediate problems behind them.
In other words, they had flown the coop.

We struck up an acquaintance with these people and instead of having them removed from the land, arranged to have them spend the winter in my cottage. It seemed like a good idea at the time.

My father had always had a fondness for poultry. He kept chickens
on Munro Street and later on Leslie Street and did rather well with this
backyard sideline, which was common practice at the time. During the
winter he had several conversations with Jock, who seemed a decent sort.
As a result of these conversations Father made a first step to getting back
into the poultry business. He bought a small roadside refreshment booth
for $10 and set it up with Jock's help. He then bought 15 laying hens,
which laid very well during the winter, assuring us and Jock and his family
of a supply of eggs.

Thus encouraged Father ordered 150 chicks to be delivered in the
spring of 1934. Jock looked after these chicks, using the brooder and
other equipment which Father had bought during the winter. By the fall
of 1934 the chicks were full grown. As I recall there were Barred Rocks,
Rhode Island Reds and some Leghorns. By November the hens were lay-
ing well and the baskets full of large white or light brown eggs seemed
to spell success and promise a return on Father's investment.

I was an innocent bystander, very respectful of my father's wishes.
If it pleased him to use the property to build up a chicken business, I saw
no objection. But the success of the enterprise was contingent upon keeping records of costs, egg production, sales and net return. This was not
done. I must say that we used many of the eggs and that Jock had his full
share, authorized and unauthorized. He also had a profitable sideline in
the disposal of the cockerels.

Jock had very little of value and most of what he had came from the
pogey. He was on relief, which meant he got chits for food, fuel and clothing. It was rather a hard way to go. He stayed at the cottage for several
seasons, gathering his firewood, helping me to gather mine and doing
chores around the place, for which I paid him.

Exactly when rifts appeared in the poultry business I do not know,
but one Sunday morning my mother asked Father at breakfast if there

were roosters with the flock. Well no, there weren't. "Well how is it then that these eggs have all been fertilized?" my mother asked. That puzzled Father and that morning he counted the hens. There were certainly fewer than there should have been. So, during a quiet Sunday afternoon chat, he asked Jock first about the fertilized eggs and then about the size of the flock. He told Jock that our customers were complaining that the eggs were not as represented but were small pullet eggs instead of the Grade A, number one eggs we said they were. Jock responded that this was ridiculous. Those people wouldn't know a fresh egg when they saw one and you had to be an expert to tell if an egg was fertilized or not. This of course convinced Father then and there that Jock was lying. As for the missing hens, well Jock presumed that foxes or skunks, or perhaps a weasel, were getting into the pens, although they were lined with tin. Father decided Jock knew more than he was telling.

On the Thursday evening following this conversation, Father and I arrived unexpectedly at the cottage to get some firewood. On the table stood a hamper containing several dozen fine looking eggs. They were beauties, just like those of the preceding fall. Jock's wife, a mild, absolutely guileless woman, suggested that we might want to take the eggs with us. Jock protested, saying it would be better to wait until Sunday, but Father took them anyway. He chuckled as we trudged back to the car over the snow, convinced that these were the eggs he should have been getting all along. But there was still another sequel in the drama that convinced him of Jock's complicity even more.

It was in the spring of the year. We were driving down Don Mills Road when we saw Jock's daughter heading toward the cottage with a large basket of eggs on her arm. Now why would she be carrying eggs to the cottage? The answer was simple. Jock had bought scruffy pullet eggs from a friend who kept poultry and passed them on to us. He then sold Father's eggs for a better price, the difference between one grade and the other being his profit.

Relations with Jock went from bad to worse, much worse. In the spring my family and I moved to the cottage for the summer and Jock and his family took up residence in a small cottage we had built on the property. During the spring and summer we got fewer and fewer eggs. It finally got to the point where with 56 hens in the coop and Father paying the feed bills, we were still buying eggs at the store. Despite the fact that we could not get our hands on a fresh, home-grown egg, Jock and his wife were seen walking away from their cottage with well-disguised baskets which screamed the presence of eggs. But the answer from Jock was always the same: there were no eggs!

One day Father came up to the cottage in a towering rage. "I can't get near that damn pen," he said "The hens have been cackling all morning and that witch is watching the pen like a crow. She must be picking up the eggs as fast as they are laid." He had had enough. Father plainly

The author's father, Joseph., standing beside poultry pen at cottage.

told Jock's wife to stay away. Jock was smart enough to stay away without being told. Father's vigil had its reward. By 11 o'clock that morning he had picked up 20 eggs. Several mornings later he gathered up 34 eggs in a single day.

The storm broke following a week of excessive heat when Jock gave Father a lecture about not paying his feed bills. While the tirade of abuse that was directed at Jock was suitably recorded at the time it seems kinder at this late date to skip it. Suffice it to say that the above recorded incident spelled the end of eggs on the Don. Father called a poultryman who bought the hens and took them away.

The poultry pen was partly demolished and the main section used to store wood. Whatever dreams Father may have had of raising poultry and selling eggs to build his retirement nest egg never materialized. All that was really salvaged from the venture was this story.

There was, in this quasi-tragic story, an amusing incident which comes readily to mind. In the course of events a rooster was added to the flock. As I recall it the bird was a plucky little creature with a black and purple plumage. Aviculturists can tell you the optimum ratio of roosters to hens, but let us say it is one rooster for every 20 hens. This rooster had to squire at least 50 grown hens. He could also exercise his powers on a few pullets that had been added to the flock along the way. The Leghorn rooster did his duty well, perhaps too well. He started tottering and staggering around the enclosure. Someone explained to me that it was rheumatism. Finally the rooster keeled over, a victim of the sad truisim of the dangers of having too much of a good thing.

Which brings me to the conclusion of this story. Having discovered what Jock was up to, it was necessary that we put up with it for a while longer. Ask anyone who has had an undesirable tenant what it takes to be rid of him. So it was with us. We went along with matters until circumstances caused the family to move on.

CHAPTER TWELVE

Sassafras, the Don Valley Goat

*I was not the only person who found in the Don Valley a country hold-
ing to which to escape from the city. The Trow family did likewise. The
Trows found their mecca on the lofty spur of the Valley wall, flanked
on the south by Pottery Road ravine and on the north and east by a steep,
shale-girded cliff at the base of which the East Don flowed. I got the
impression, while standing on the summit of Trow Hill, of being on an
oasis of wooded land, cut away from the rest of the Valley, and of course
from the city as well.*

*In those days Broadview and Danforth Avenues were a fairly
lengthy walk from Trow Hill. This was hard on Mrs. Trow, for she did
much of the shopping on foot. There was no bus service along Broadview Avenue at the time. There were still parts of the original Todmorden Mills village back of Bater's General Store on Broadview Avenue.
Several of the families living in houses off Broadview drew water from
a common tap near Bater's Store. Bater's was a general store and a post
office, where we bought stamps and picked up our mail. This was in
1939 and for quite a number of years after! The better-known customers
not only bought groceries but spent a half hour or so discussing poli-
tics and other topics of the day.*

*It was through the kindness of the Trows that Old Murph, the bee-
man, was permitted to keep bees at the base of their hill. The site is still
visible from Pottery Road where it crosses the CNR line. Through Murph
I became acquainted with the Trows and took my small daughters for
walks through the red oak woodlands that covered the top of the hill.
That is how I learned about goats and how I was able, every once in
a while, to buy a few quarts of goat's milk. Eventually we kept a goat
of our own by the name of Sassafras; Sass for short and what a poor
choice she was.*

*The building of the Bayview extension put an end to Trow Hill, that
is to most of it. The Trow estate fell to the bulldozer of progress. Today
Trow Hill is a memory and the Pottery Road ravine severed and
sequestered, cut off by the incessant traffic on the Bayview extension.*

In the 1930s Pottery Road continued north of the CNR line, skirting the edge of a steep hill of a well-wooded ravine, the remnants of which may still be seen. It was at the base of this lofty hill, facing the railway, that Old Murph, the beekeeper, kept his apiary. There was a long winding back way to the top of the hill, but the most direct route, which also led from Murph's, was by several flights of steep stairs, which tested a person's legs and wind.

I called the steep prong in the Valley wall Trow Hill, as it was owned by Dr. and Mrs. Alan Trow. The crest of the hill was isolated from the rest of the Valley. While walking through the glades of red oak trees, or along the path which skirted the crest of the hill and the winding Don, you got the impression that here was an oasis. You felt cut off from the turmoil of the city, even though it lay just beyond Pottery Road. Alas, the crest has since largely disappeared to provide a route for the Bayview extension.

Before I knew them the Trows had happened upon this oasis, liked it immensely and bought it. They built a cement block house with a flat roof which, as I recall, was furnished with elegant taste and was very comfortable. The Trows, especially Mrs. Trow and the children, seemed very happy there. After Murph's introduction, I would visit the Trows on occasion. They kept a small herd of goats and I bought goat's milk from them on occasion. As I already bought honey from Murph, the Valley was for me at one time a land overflowing with (goat's) milk and honey.

The goats, who were obviously spoiled pets, answered to a collection of names, some of which I recall: Jeannie, the Kid, and Sassafras. I continued to buy goat's milk until one spring Mrs. Trow said, "Why don't you take one of the goats to your cottage for the summer. It will give you a supply of milk." I fell in with the idea and a goat was chosen for me.

Mrs. Trow selected Sassafras, who she described as a mature milker. It appeared that "Sass" did not get along too well with her sisters so a holiday for her seemed like a good idea. My wife and father liked the idea of a goat so we picked up Sass, stuffed her in the car valise and quickly transported her the two miles to my cottage up Valley from Trow Hill.

Had I been in Sass's place I would have reasonsed that there was cause for great rejoicing. Being conveyed to an area rich and lush with clover and succulent grasses, where a goat could nibble at will under the eyes of loving caretakers, should have appealed to any goat.

Very pleased that Sass had fallen on such good fortune, we tied her to the end of a long rope and led her to a choice place on the property. Here she could nibble at will and forget the frustrations of having had to live with her sisters. That was the beginning of the end of a beautiful relationship. Sass began to stampede, to bleat, "bla, bla, bla," and to become hopelessly entangled in the rope. Sass had decided to be lonesome right away and bla-blahed incessantly. Father and I went over, disentangled Sass and freed her to nibble at the clover, whereupon the whole charade

Sassafras with author's daughters. Denise left, Monique right. circa 1939.

started all over again. We were all frustrated and Sass spent her first night at our place in the workshop.

Our first attempts at milking Sass, which was the whole point of the exercise, were not entirely successful. I anticipated that Sass would have been well indoctrinated in the process of milking but such was not the case. The milk flowed freely and filled the small pail provided for the purpose. But at the precise moment I picked up the full pail, Sass kicked it over. After a few days of this sort of thing we stood Sass on the lawn table, whereupon Father held her by the rear feet and horns and either my wife or I would do the milking. At least we got the milk, which at first was very creamy and rich. And there was lots of it.

But gradually, as our acquaintance with Sass broadened, we began to learn a few things about her and suspect much more. Sass had been grain fed so while there was an abundance of clover, vetch, wild pea, grass and other dainties on our place, she simply would not touch them. Sass wanted a dish of oats. It also dawned on us that Sass and her sisters had been fed their own milk, a practice that she felt should be continued at the Forks of the Don and upon which I frowned. It also became apparent that Mrs. Trow had pampered the goats. They had made free and easy around the Trow holdings and Sass expected the same treatment at the cottage. It was necessary on one occasion to eject the bearded Sass from our kitchen.

Sass also clung to every opportunity to be in the vicinity of the cottage and when en route to pasture, stalled and had to be dragged very much against her will. The rope continued to be a problem. Countless times she became entangled in it and we had to untangle her. There was a peculiar "bla" that told us that Sass was in trouble again. While this was going on Sass, of course, was not eating, which meant that she was not producing milk.

I tried putting her on the other side of the fence but when the horses a neighbouring farmer let loose on the Flats came near, Sass stampeded and ran into the fence. Finally I gave in and quartered her in a comfortable pen by the river bank with room to roam. I brought her great bunches of clover and other sweet smelling crops of the Valley but to no avail. She simply would not touch this fodder. Finally the best advice came from Father. He said, "That goat isn't used to greens. Give her a good dish of oats mixed with wet bran twice a day. That will bring her along." I did. Sass nearly knocked me over in her eagerness to get at the tempting dish and lapped up the oats and bran in quick order. From then on Sass got her dish of oats and bran twice a day.

Sass wouldn't touch water either. We just could not make her drink, which was distressing to me as I assumed that a waterless goat was a milk-less goat. But the solution was eventually driven home: Sass wanted stronger brew. She and her sisters had been given their own milk to drink because at the Trow's home, water was in short supply and goat's milk was plentiful.

During the summer Sass's production dropped from one and a half quarts a day to less than a quart per day. But the milk we got was something that made me prefer it to all other and convinced me that the goat had been rightfully called the poor man's cow.

During our occasional visits that summer to Trow Hill I got the impression that Sass was more than a loan. I suspected that she was a gift and that Mrs. Trow felt that we were going to keep her. However the day came when, with summer's end in sight and our return to the city imminent, Sass had to be returned to her true owner. Accordingly she was taken back to Trow Hill. Mrs. Trow was visibly disappointed when she learned that this was not a social call and that Sass had come back to stay. I remember the occasion well. Sass, on finding her four feet on the crest of the hill, began to paw the ground. At that moment I saw a massive goat, much heavier than Sass, walking slowly along the path overlooking the river, head down. It was Jeannie, Sass's arch rival and sworn enemy, equipped with a formidable set of horns. She spotted Sass from afar but still came on slowly, with head bowed. Sass broke more ground and lowered her horns for what was to come.

The two rivals were now close to each other. Jeannie raised her horns and brought them down on Sass's smaller horns with a resounding whack. There was some jostling, shoving and pushing, whereupon Jeannie broke away to raise herself for another downward attack on Sass's

Don Valley farm horses.

head. Her driving power was awesome and such was the force of this second blow that Sass crumpled to her knees. From then on Sass fought a defensive and losing fight. With each fresh lunge Jeannie raised herself higher and higher. In an almost erect position, she would give her hind legs a kick, her horns a twist and the incensed goat would land on Sass's head. Just as Jeannie was preparing for the knockout butt, Sass did a wise thing: she left the field of battle. A few days later Mrs. Trow sold her to a country man.

CHAPTER THIRTEEN

A Garden of Earthly Delights

It was a distinct pleasure to reread the following chapter months after I had written it in draft form. It brought back the good old days, when my gardens were one of the joys of my life. Some people are reputed to have been born with a silver spoon in their mouths. If such things are possible, I was undoubtedly born with a package of garden seeds in mine.

Thanks to Providence, time and, in some measure common sense, I do not bother now with a fruit and vegetable garden, although I did north of Tweed until 1975. Why, you may ask did I as a young man concern myself with gardens at all, when so many other pursuits beckoned? I was a lover of the soil and a fervent believer in its productivity. Furthermore the call of my ancestors was strong within me. Then again, there was much less for a young man to do than there is today.

Planting the garden was an event I looked forward to each year. Almost as soon as Christmas was over I started planning the garden. By the time the seed catalogues came out, wisely planned for February, I was ready to go. Those colourful catalogues shortened the winter and were amazing in the way they were able to tell an oft-repeated tale as though it was all brand new. Half the fun in gardening was perusing the catalogues and then buying the required seeds and nursery stock.

I still savour the sheer joy of buying my fruit tree stock from Hogg's Nursery in Uxbridge. Planting those trees in newly turned over garden soil and watching them bear fruit from year to year was one of the biggest pleasures of my stay on the Don.

The fruit and vegetable gardens yielded well, with only a few minor concerns such as potato bugs. You had to watch the crows of course, because they would pull up the seed corn as fast as it was put in. but you could foil them by mixing roofing tar with sand in a can, placing the seed corn in it and swishing everything around until the seed was covered with the tar and sand. Believe me the crows never touched it.

Today, as many gardeners will affirm, garden plots are beset with an array of pests of which groundhogs are foremost. Yet in the '20s and '30s I never saw a groundhog, or at least one that preferred raiding my garden to staying at home. There were many foxes around in those days and groundhogs were part of the food chain for foxes. The same with

94

raccoons, they took the odd cob of corn but busied themselves mostly with catching crayfish, minnows, frogs and other raccoon delicacies available from the Don and adjacent wetlands. The raccoons and groundhogs were in balance with their surroundings, but not today.

When the Don Valley Parkway went through the Valley all this was changed. One summer I live-trapped 30 groundhogs on the one-acre de Grassi lot. In November there were still groundhogs emerging from their dens. These migrants kept filling the dens as quickly as they were evacuated.

My garden died when I realized that we could not use the produce. I had become much busier, and perhaps wiser, and I no longer had access to a garden in the Don Valley. Perhaps I simply grew out of gardens. But let me tell you that there is just nothing to equal the recollection of that hand-operated tractor churning over the sleek, black, odorous, winter-washed soil and its topping of horse manure, especially on a sunny spring day when Nature is alive with joy.

One of my perennial accomplishments during my stay at the Forks of the Don were the fruit and vegetable gardens. The notion of a garden was probably inherited from my parents who, for as long as I could remember, made gardens within the limits of small backyard space. In 1928, when I acquired my Don acreage, I had more land than I could be reasonably expected to deal with, all things considered.

There were the remains of an orchard when I came on the place; decrepit old apple trees, veterans of bygone days, whose value to me over the years was in the dead wood I pruned from them each spring. There had been a garden plot at one time too. The first spring Father and I started turning over the twitch grass ready for planting potatoes, which was a way of getting rid of the twitch. This sort of thing was carried on for several seasons, with good results.

My acreage skirted the Don River on one side and the boundary line on the other side was pasture. I enclosed part of the property with a fence and within this enclosure I planted 24 fruit trees. There were plum, cherry, apple and pear trees. Over the years these trees yielded satisfactory crops, despite my failings in the techniques of fruit spraying. Concurrently with the fruit trees I began to buy raspberry canes, black and red currant bushes and strawberry plants, along with several clumps of rhubarb. Nursery catalogues were one of the pitfalls in my life. Their glowing descriptions of their stock and the superb photography led me many a time, figuratively speaking, down the garden path. The names were as full of meaning as the fruit, Latham, Everbearing, Cuthbert. And they all lived up to expectation.

The Forks of the Don was an ideal place for small fruits, with just the right combination of light soil, humidity from the river, abundant sunshine and protection provided by the lofty Valley walls. Fertilizing was required but it was taken care of by Hastings Dairy who had quarters on Broadview Avenue across from Fulton Avenue. In those days milk was delivered by horse-drawn vehicles. Of course this meant stables and manure. By arrangement, one of the local farmers would stop off at Hastings Dairy on his return to the city with an empty truck and load it up with manure. He would then deliver the manure to my garden for a few dollars.

Eventually the orchard and fruit garden appeared as they had been planned on paper. The trees were planted at regular intervals, with the fruit bushes in rows between them a hundred feet long and more. It never occurred to me that there could be a large reward for my husbandry but there was certainly enough work to do – manuring, cultivating, pruning, weeding and eventually picking the fruit.

The fruit garden was the start. I believed that all the land should be put to good use. In February I spent hours pouring over the pages of the seed catalogues. A steady stream of packages of seeds from the local seed houses and the mail order houses poured through the mailbox. In the late twenties and thirties the seed houses in Toronto were all grouped on King Street East, between Church and Jarvis, most of them on the south side. They included Rennies, Steele Briggs, Webbs, Keiths and I recall Carter's and Simmers there at one time or another. The stores were an emporium where seed buffs, like myself, wandered in from the adjacent office buildings to spend their noon hour making purchases. Then there were the mail order houses, of which Dominion Seed Co. was emerging as a force to be reckoned with. Their vegetable novelties were so glowingly described that one could scarcely resist them. By early April, with the ground scarcely released from winter, I was ready to put in the first radish rows. I was in good company, for in the late twenties what is now the north side of O'Connor Drive between Pape and Woodbine was largely in market gardens.

For several summers the garden prospered with radishes, lettuce, carrots, cucumbers, cabbage, corn, string beans, peas, turnips, potatoes and a few other vegetables following in sequence. Usually everything went as planned and many times I took home hampers of vegetables, which my mother was glad to have.

Eventually I purchased a small gasoline tractor, a sort of homemade thing produced locally but very serviceable. It came with an assortment of interchangeable equipment and could be used for plowing, discing and scuffling. It released me from the bondage of turning over the soil a forkful at a time. It was sheer luxury to operate that tractor through the fruit rows and do in minutes what would otherwise have taken hours.

In 1933 I made a deal with Steele Briggs. They gave me some garden tools in exchange for a full page ad in a trade paper on which I was working at the time. The tools were made in England and I still have several

Fine view of author's garden and orchard at Forks of the Don.

of them today, as sound as the day I got them. One is a long narrow spade with which I have planted tens of thousands of seedling trees and still do so annually in the Don Valley with the Outing Club of East York.

Up until the time of my acquisition of the tractor I was still in charge of the situation. But as I have learned in life, certain challenges become obsessions with me. This time it was the fence line. It bothered me that my garden had not quite reached the fence line. Not that it needed to. I was merely obsessed with the notion that all the land should be brought into production. So one spring I decided that I was going to reach that objective or bust. I worked my way foot by foot to that fence line and, having mastered the soil, proceeded to set out the seeds in rows. Soon green pencilled lines of radishes, beets and carrots emerged.

By then my garden domain had become a time-consuming monster with all the weeding, hoeing and raking that needed to be done. After a while I began to sag and to experience a feeling of weariness and almost hopelessness that takes hold of all of us at times. I knew the symptoms: I had been overreaching myself. A wonderful hobby had been turned into a backbreaking chore.

It was one of those placid evenings in mid-May that I remember so well. The sad trilling of the American toads echoed intermittently from the frog pond across the way. It is a call like none other in nature that epitomizes the hushed quiet of a spring evening. I was alone at the time, weary from my efforts. Seated on a bench that commanded a view of my kingdom, I could see the fruit trees, the corn, the potato patch, the strawberry bed, the raspberry canes and currant bushes, the rank and file of the vegetable rows. It was all there, all mine.

Looking out at this scene I reached a momentous decision. I rose from the bench, walked to the workshop and got down a hoe. Then, with the slow pace of a *sans culotte* of the French Revolution escorting a cart full of victims to the guillotine, I marched with the hoe on my shoulder through the garden to the newly-conquered lands near the fence line. Methodically I ran the hoe over the emerging rows of vegetables. It was murder. In minutes the fresh green rows, so full of promise, disappeared in a welter of raked-over soil. A half hour later the job was done. I had destroyed half of my vegetable garden, not without a sense of loss, but sadly admitting the futility of going too far.

An hour later when my wife returned to the cottage, I told her what had happened. She inquired after my reasons, already knowing full well why. I said, "Before you left I was a slave to that garden. Now I am master once more." It was a valuable lesson for a person of my temperament. What may have seemed like a childish act served me well in setting a pattern where discipline was the password on occasions when situations emerged that were much more complex than the length of a few rows of vegetable seedlings.

For the last 15 years I have been unable to grow a black currant bush that produced fruit. Not one! This despite my efforts to buy good stock and to research black currant behaviour. However at the Forks of the Don it was a different matter. At the zenith of my gardening days I had 60 black currant bushes, which in their third year of growth were producing heavy crops of fruit. The average person will not know what this means without having had a comparable experience. It means that a black currant bush is covered with fruit, but fruit that ripens gradually over a period of time. Accordingly the gardener can anticipate picking fruit for several weeks. I tried every recipe and learned that there were only so many black currants that a family man could use. So I called in friends, who brought more friends, and still there was no end to the harvest, with the result that much of the fruit was wasted on the bushes. Again I solved the problem with draconian measures. I simply pulled up half the stock. What a pity that was.

Under these circumstances I marvel unceasingly at the productivity of nature when left alone or encouraged to proceed in a normal manner. At the same time it saddens me that so many of the things of which we are deprived in terms of fruit and vegetables could be easily grown in sufficient quantity.

CHAPTER FOURTEEN

A Taste of Summer

In retrospect I wonder why I ever bought a canning machine. Perhaps because it was a novelty, easily available, in keeping with the times and in tune with my ideas.

It all started with my travels in the province of Quebec, where I observed that home canning outfits seemed to be standard equipment in every farm home. The farm folk were dependent upon them and canned great quantities of tomatoes, peas, beans, other vegetables and some meats. In the course of events I made friends with two families who came from rural Quebec and they knew all about canning machines.

I had a large garden on my property at the Forks of the Don and I reasoned that if I bought a canning machine I could certainly put it to good use.

The canning machine was built to last a thousand years, which means that I still have it stored away in my workshop against a future need, which may be no more serious than to exhibit it as a relic.

Yet at the time it was important to have one. It seemed so practical to grow things and to extend the availability of the crops I had grown into the winter. Imagine, home-grown strawberries, raspberries, tomatoes and corn on the shelves to recall, amid the blasts of winter, the pleasant days of gardening in the sun.

The notion that I should own a home canning machine was arrived at in a roundabout way. During the Depression, Canadian National Railways closed its St. Malo operations. Many of the men employed in the repair shops there were transferred to the Leaside shops, where they were engaged in repairing cabooses.

I became acquainted with several of these men, first Amede Hamel and later Joe Giguere. They were stalwart fellows who had pioneered in the Abitibi region of Quebec, worked in lumber camps and on the railroad and who knew what life on the thin edge was all about. We became firm friends. They helped me on my few acres and showed me the tricks of the outdoor trade – how to use a crosscut saw, how to split pine knots, how to fell a leaning tree against the lean and much more.

The Hamels lived on Broadview Avenue near Cosburn. Mrs. Hamel looked after the children sometimes. Being country folk at heart, they took to my acres at the Forks of the Don with the excitement of a gosling reaching water for the first time. The Hamels, and later the Gigueres, had gardens of their own on my land and produced some of the largest potatoes I have ever seen. There was an abundance of land for gardening beyond what I ever wanted to use and I was glad to see these people make the most of it.

During one of our visits, Amede Hamel said to me, "Monsieur Charles," (He always addressed me that way.) "You should have *une sertisseuse*." Translated that means a home canning machine. He proceeded to explain how practical and useful it was. "There is one in use on most of the farms in Quebec," he said. "People can fruit, vegetables and meats with them. It is a great waste not to have one."

I became interested, did some shopping around and had one shipped to me via Canada Steamship Lines along with a five gallon drum of table molasses. The canning machine, which I still have, is as good as the day I bought it for $14. Getting cans for it was no problem. These could be ordered in any size or quantity from the American Can Co., along with the lids, for an average cost of two cents per can and lid. They were shipped in huge cardboard containers, which jingled incessantly when opened.

It was a simple matter to operate the machine. A can was placed in position on a steel plate. An overhead lever brought a second steel plate in position over the unsealed lid. A lever was pressed against the flanges and thus sealed the can. Cans could be re-flanged and recycled or kept to store screws, bolts, nails or small hardware.

Our first summer canning our garden's produce under Hamel's approving eyes was a success. We put down 250 cans of fruit and vegetables and subsequently salvaged 245 cans. Our stock included strawberries, raspberries, cherries, plums, apple sauce, peaches and pineapples, the latter two purchased at the fruit market. Vegetables included tomatoes, string beans, both green and yellow, and corn.

Our adventures in canning are something I recall with kindly thoughts. We had the perfect procedure for the venture. Brine was prepared for the vegetables and syrup for the fruit. When a stock of either had been sealed, the cans were placed in my 30-gallon maple syrup evaporator. This sat on an open top stove so that the bottom of the nickel-plated evaporator became the top of the stove. A swing door made it possible to fill the grate with three-foot lengths of wood. Once the fire was lit the water in the evaporator came to a boil in a matter of minutes.

The fruit was left for 20 minutes, the vegetables for several hours. I recall my concern when I was awakened during the night following the preparation of our first batch of cans. Suddenly there was a strident "pop", then "pop, pop, pop". It sounded like the report of a rifle. I came downstairs, fully expecting to find that the cans had exploded, but such was not the case. The cans had been set on the kitchen table to cool off and it was the deflation of the heat-bulged edges of the cans that had produced the alarming sounds.

I was quick to perceive that wild black cap raspberries could be included in the canning program. The black cap is actually a wild black raspberry, succulent at one point in its growth but seedy if left too long on the cane. The slope adjacent to my fence line was literally covered with them. Roots producing fruit bearing canes for the first time bore very large black caps and the canes could be stripped quickly.

It was customary for us, that is my wife, two small daughters and I, to climb the fence after dinner and spend an hour or two gathering black caps. We often returned from our forays with sufficient fruit to fill 12 large cans. By 9 o'clock in the evening the cans were sealed, the contents boiled and ready for future use. Not too many people can record a similar experience.

I have since visited the slope many times but today scarcely a black cap cane can be seen. They, like the thimbleberry stands, have a tendency to peter out and start up elsewhere. This is done largely through nature's own mechanism for renewing stock, such as a seed dropped by birds. Be that as it may, there are comparatively few black caps at the Forks of the Don today.

During the Depression, family groups were often seen ranging the Flats picking raspberries. There were some magnificent stands of wild raspberries along the Don, if a person knew where to find them. On one occasion the land under the hydro lines traversing the Valley was burnt over, which left a thick layer of potash and ashes on the soil. The following year the raspberry canes produced huge berries. That summer I spent several afternoons in that area picking berries, completely cut off fron the outside world by tall raspberry canes.

People may well wonder why we bothered to can at all, given that we had so much within easy reach. The Depression was in full swing. The economy was such that the government encouraged initiatives to supplement the food supply. My diary of the time throws some light on my attitudes with respect to canning.

> *"My interest in canning went deeper. Through it, we were a little more self reliant, or self sufficient than without the canning machine, less dependent on the corner store. This had been accomplished through the purchase of a mechanism at a cost of $14 and a stock of cans at a cost of two cents each.*
>
> *"Everything we needed for canning was within reach, even the wood which heated the water, and the water that came from the well. A canning machine will help anyone who is trying to live off the land."*

Some 50 years later I reconginze that the reason for our success at canning rested with my wife, Simonne, who masterminded the operation with consummate skill. She was the person on whom everything depended.

As we moved through our second year of homemade canned goods it became obvious that we were top-heavy with raspberries and strawberries in particular. These were nice to have but at times I yearned for a dish of good old fashioned prunes or apricots. Very gradually we found less and less need for the things we had canned. The pressure to keep on canning lessened and gradually we gave it up.

The vegetable juicer made its appearance at my cottage concurrently with the canning machine. It was operated on the same principle as a meat grinder and, while it could not be compared with the power-driven juicers in use today, it did a good job as far as it went. We put tomatoes, cucumbers, rhubarb, celery and apples through the juicer. The vegetable pulp left over from the juicing seemed a bit of a waste, but most of our juicing was done in the fall when there was an abundance of everything. I drank more vegetable juice at that time than at any time since. This was pure juice, fresh from the garden, and most appetizing when seasoned with salt. It was about that time that canned vegetable juice first made its appearance on grocery store shelves. I often recall the delights of sipping a glass of tomato, apple, celery or cucumber juice and thinking of it as a high point of gracious living.

Rhubarb juice was something else. Sometimes we served it diluted half and half with water with a pinch of baking soda added. We called it rhubarb fizz and its effect at times went far beyond the appetizer it was meant to be. We also tried rhubarb juice straight, heavily sweetened with honey and served ice cold.

I experimented with the pit method of preserving apples and carrots. This required a pit four feet deep in a convenient location. The pit was filled with loose straw and apples or carrots were dumped on top. The top of the pit was then sealed over with straw or leaves and mounded with earth. Thus secured against the weather, the contents of the pit mellowed. It was a great way to get the best out of Spy apples, which are always tart in the fall. The confinement mellowed them.

One fall I filled a pit with Spys and Delicious apples. It was late February before I got around to breaking into the pit. Much to my surprise I found nothing, despite much rustling around in the straw. Unconvinced, I tried again and again but to no avail. There was no fruit there. Every last apple had disappeared. I never mentioned this to the one person whom I felt knew the answer, as the reply would have been, "Well, I guess the rats or the mice or the raccoons got them." It was too small an incident to make an issue of but it spoke volumes about this person.

The other pit incident is a different kind of story. I had built a small but neat little root house into a slope on the de Grassi property. It was

Eric LaTrobe removing apples from pit at rear of author's cottage, 1938. New tree planting now a grove of large trees.

just big enough for me to enter on all fours and deep enough to escape the frost. That fall I filled it with carrots and used quite a number of them during the winter. But come spring, I opened the door to the root house one day to find a litter of four raccoons toddling around among the carrots. I had a decision to make and opted to leave the raccoons with the rest of the carrots.

The cottage also had a cellar. Its walls were made of river gravel mixed with cement. The temperature in the cellar at all times was just right, both in summer and winter. Prior to our purchase of an ice box, milk could be kept fresh in the cellar for several days.

In due course I cleaned out the cellar and whitewashed the walls. A carpenter built bins and shelves to hold my crops of potatoes, apples, carrots and turnips. Spy apples mellowed here particularly well. It was a pleasant experience to spend an hour on a cold winter day rummaging in the bins, secure from the weather, gathering the week's supply of vegetables which I would carry over the snow covered ground to my car. In my imagination I was still gardening, albeit below the frost line. It was a treat to select a stout cabbage or to shake loose the sand from the carrots which, along with the apples, exuded the scent of summer.

In its own way the root cellar told of the approach of spring, or rather the wearing away of winter. In time the cabbages disintegrated, especially the summer kind, the rutabagas and the carrots began to sprout foliage and the potatoes developed eyes. There seemed to be an irresistible force that prompted them to do this. It was a signal that winter was on the wane. It always struck me as odd that the cellar could be so secure from the rigours of winter. It was never heated but the vegetables wintered well, escaping the frost. In truth, because of it, we were never far from summer.

CHAPTER FIFTEEN

Freshets, Floods and Bridges

The Don River, as I learned, was temperamental, its mood dependant upon the level of the water and the climatic conditions that governed it. My property, with the exception of the de Grassi lot, was on the east bank of the Don, which meant that I had to cross the river to reach the bulk of my holdings. My situation was similar to the person who has to reach a cottage on an island in a lake by small boat; everything had to be transported piecemeal. I built several bridges, which was probably the most expensive, time-consuming and eventually futile effort of my years in the Valley. In time I discovered that a bridge slung on cables solved my problem.

It takes a fair measure of determination to put up with this sort of inconvenience. Nevertheless it seemed worth it at the time. Today I put it all down to experience. It has often been said regarding travel that half the fun is in getting there. In owning property, all of the fun, in my view, is in getting there – easily. to be able to drive a car within feet of one's door, now that's fun!

Despite its shortcomings the Forks of the Don left me with at least one claim to fame, namely being the person who probably built more bridges in that area than anyone else since the land was first cleared.

Four of my five acres at the Forks of the Don were across the river from Don Mills Road. The one land access to them was via a wooden bridge over Taylor Creek. Once across this bridge I could drive or walk along the flood plain to my holdings. I was in a legal position when I used this route for a right of way over it had been included in the transaction when John Hawthorne Taylor sold the land, which I eventually bought, to Canadian Northern Railways.

The Taylor Creek bridge had been a handsome structure in its prime but it had greatly deteriorated after the flood of 1939. The superstructure had been severely damaged by water. The people who used the bridge to reach their farm above the Valley solved the problem of bridge maintenance by knocking away the superstructure. From then on we crossed on the two pine logs and planks that constituted the floor of the bridge. To make matters worse, trucks loaded with swill were driven over

Bridge over Taylor's Creek, Forks of the Don., circa 1920.

the bridge several times a day. A bridge will stand only so much of this. Once I took matters into my own hands and made some repairs to the planking. But I could not stand for this sort of thing very long and sought alternative access to my place.

I often left my car on the de Grassi property and walked across a footbridge which was easily set up for summer and fall use. But I wanted something better. Then I learned that we could actually drive across the river if I cleared the river stones and smoothed the gravel from one shore to the other. This was fine as long as the river stayed at normal summer level. But the Don was absolutely unpredictable. It could rise in the night and make the ford impassable the next morning.

In my early days at the Forks I forded the river quite easily, even at spring level, by wearing a pair of "Light and tough" hip waders. On occasion I waded into the river with a companion on my back who doubted he would reach the other bank without having first sat in the water. The conquest of the Forks of the Don was not without its lighter moments.

Our first serious attempt at bridge building was a pier that could withstand anything, or so we thought at the time. We spent one summer building that pier. We rented a local horse by the name of Lady and a stone boat. The rib work of the pier was made of railway ties spiked together and filled with river stones scooped up by the stone boat. The pier was a formidable affair, at least in appearance, as it was sheathed in metal. Just how we were going to use the pier had not been defined, which was just

Bridge at the Forks of the Don built in 1921.

as well. The following spring, during river breakup, the ice smashed the pier to bits and scattered the stone along the river bottom.

I actually walked across the second bridge we built, stood in the middle of it, looked up and down the Don and admired what seemed to be a very good piece of construction. Built by a carpenter, the bridge consisted of two holding beams, several piers and a plank floor. It cost me a few dollars. All I had to do was drive the car to the back of the de Grassi place and go across the bridge to the cottage. I did this once. The bridge was built to last 50 years in Florida but lasted one night on the unpredictable Don.

It was late May. We were past the flood season and although it had rained during the week, the effect of the rain on the river was not noticeable. But during the night the water rose several feet and by dawn the bridge had disappeared. When I stepped out of the cottage in the morning there was no sign of it. Brokenhearted, I set out with the carpenter in search of the remains. Luckily the entire bridge, minus the piers, had been caught in the shrubbery near Todmorden Park. The wood was salvaged and brought back in a truck. All that work and expense, though, went for nothing.

It was maddening to learn later that the rise in the water level could have been avoided. There was a large dam on the Don, upstream at Donalda. Instead of letting the water out gradually, someone had simply opened the sluice and released the water in a torrent. When it reached

Cable bridge connecting the author's two properties at Forks of the Don, circa 1948. Bridge swept away by Hurricane Hazel.

the bridge the great flow lifted it off its piers and floated it downstream. The power of water is awesome. A person has to live through an experience like this to appreciate the frustration it can give rise to. I swore, as men of good faith swear, that never again would I be subjugated to the whims of an idiot.

The next exercise in bridge building resulted in a cable bridge, which served me well until the night of Hurricane Hazel. A craftsman by the name of Emile Landry, who could work like any two men or more, put it together. I have described this bridge in detail elsewhere in my writings so a few lines will suffice here. Four cables were stretched from a clump of willows on the de Grassi bank to two steel rails sunk in the sand and protected by a huge metal drum filled with sand. The cables were laid cantilever style, with a wooden basket serving as a cradle in the middle. There were two cables at the top and two at the bottom of the basket. The bottom of the cradle was three feet closer to the Don than the floor of the bridge and this bothered me. But the cables cleared all flood waters until the night of Hurricane Hazel. On that occasion the Don rose to an unprecedented level and with such force that the cables were torn from their moorings at one end. The entire bridge was flung to the cottage shore of the Don.

I tried again, right after Hurricane Hazel. Within six weeks a second cable bridge had been erected on the assumption that there would not

Rare old print of freight train coming down the Don before Viaduct opened. Photo circa 1917. Present Bayview extension replaced railway in this location. Castle Frank location upper left of photo.

be another Hazel in a hundred years. This time Landry outdid himself. He raised the cables five feet above the level of the previous bridge. Steps on each side of the bridge were used to reach the floor of the bridge. The bridge was a masterepiece, and so high, 15 feet above the water, as to require handrails on each side. This time the cables were suspended from hydro poles and gripped together in the centre. There was no understructure cantilever effect. Any flood waters would have to be very high to reach the bridge floor. The final touch was an electric switch at each end of the bridge so that we could turn on or shut off flood lights when crossing or leaving the bridge. I called it the "Emile Landry bridge". I doubt if there has ever been anything like it on the Don, built by one man using run-of-the-mill materials. There is a swing bridge in Sunnybrook Park, built for pedestrian traffic, but it is a highly professional job that probably cost a thousand times more than the cable bridge at the Forks of the Don.

Having built this bridge to last forever I lived to see the day, ten years later, when it was demolished on my instructions by the man who had built it. By then my property across the Don had been expropriated for the Don Valley Parkway and I had moved over to the de Grassi place. Furthermore the youth of the day spent hours trying to swing the bridge off its moorings, which was a hazard both to them and to me, so I simply had it taken down. All that is left today of this considerable effort are the two steel rails which are still to be seen above the sand and the steel drum that served as a buttress against long-forgotten flood waters. *Requiem in pace.*

Fifty or more years ago the spring breakup of the river ice was sensational. In those days the blocks were three or more feet thick. There are no spring breakups on the Don today to compare with those of the twenties and thirties. These usually occurred in the wake of an all night rain in late March or early April. The ice floes would start to heave and shove like so many battering rams. It was a spectacle of piled-up ice floes, 30 or more feet in circumference, engaged in mortal combat, each endeavouring to strangle the other in the general panic to be free of the river and to hurry on to the lake.

If we were lucky the best of the show occurred in daytime. If it happened on a Saturday it was worth it to sit by the river bank, high up of course, and watch the swift movements of the floes in a steady procession, jostling each other. It provided evidence that winter was definitely over. The big floes were followed by smaller stuff. The debris which it carried with it was the flotsam of the season: household equipment, coops, barn wood and of course the trees, branches and logs. Much of this could be fished out of the river with my 15-foot pike pole. I long at times for the entertainment of a good old fashioned spring freshet, but alas, with warmer water and development which precludes thick ice, they are no more along the Don.

Floods were a different matter. There were ordinary floods and serious ones, like the flood of 1929 and Hurricane Hazel in 1954. Hurricane Hazel was the worst. It has already been described in detail so I won't mention it further, except to say that it ruined all of the garden soil on my property. The flood in the spring of 1929 caught us off guard. As the Don rose, men worked through the night, cutting down the willows along the bank in an attempt to stave off the flood. They were lucky when the flood abated of its own accord. The gaping holes left in the flooded river bank were filled in with old automobile bodies. These constituted the most objectionable sight on the Don for years until successive ice breakups battered the rusted metal into a compact mass, which is still there today.

As an aside to this story, Bill Skelhorne kept pigs on the de Grassi property at the time of the 1929 flood. The end of the piggery hugged the bank close to the river. Several years after the 1929 flood, East York passed a by-law prohibiting the raising of pigs in the municipality. The people engaged in this business moved out and several of them went to Wexford, arriving just before the building boom. They all became wealthy men as a result. My reward from all this was to be able to clean up the de Grassi lot once and for all.

After Hurricane Hazel passed through, more great gaping holes appeared in the river bank beyond the area filled with automobile bodies. During the summer following the hurricane, the municipality of East

Charlie Bell (left) and Bill Skelhorne (right). Skelhorne kept several hundred pigs in East York until about 1930 when pig raising was prohibited by law in Toronto.

York trucked in broken pieces of sidewalk, something like 42 truck loads. The holes were filled and the concrete slabs may be seen to this day.

Back to the subject of bridges, I well recall the wooden trestle bridge on de Grassi Hill that conveyed traffic over the Canadian National Railway line. De Grassi Hill had a steep grade and was paved with red paving bricks. It was a lung tester for anyone who tried to ride a bicycle up the hill. It was a challenge too for automobile engines and brakes. A one-legged veteran of the First World War who lost control of his car was killed when he crashed through the guard rails onto the railway.

Another bridge spanned the Don at the foot of de Grassi Hill in the early '20s. it had a plank-covered floor supported by steel girders. We always broke step when crossing it in a group because of the sway. It was replaced in the late twenties by the cement arch bridge which is still there today.

One can no longer see the massive bulk of Tumper's Hill, which was directly in line with the south end of the cement arch bridge. The bridge was built facing directly into Tumper's Hill and there was a T-square or a hairpin turn at the end of the bridge. There was no way of telling when you crossed the bridge if a car was coming from the opposite direction. Some said that Tumper's Hill would someday be removed to bring the bridge into a direct line with Coxwell Avenue. For a few years, as traffic grew, the bridge was a real hazard and many a fender met its end on that hairpin turn. Even today the buttresses are pock-marked as a result of innumerable scrapings from close shaves.

One particular incident comes readily to mind. A milk truck was returning from a scheduled run, laden with cans full of milk. Its brakes gave out on de Grassi Hill and the truck rolled down the hill at a merry clip. It rounded the hairpin turn on two wheels, slammed into Tumper's Hill and rolled on its side, spilling milk freely in the ditch. Providentially no other vehicle was on the road at the time.

Tumper's Hill as I knew it has quite disappeared. It was bulldozed in order to provide cheap fill for the Don Valley Parkway. While I was writing this story I met a chap by the name of Edmonds who had fought a hard battle to save it. He showed me photographs of the mount and its summit which are collector's items today. It can only be concluded sadly that the public lost an incomparable site for hiking and trail skiing.

Yet another bridge spanned the West Don River at the Forks and could be seen from the cement arch bridge. It too has a story. It was gracefully built (see the picture in *Remembering the Don*, p. 135). Its initial purpose was to provide access from the community at the Forks of the Don to Thorncliffe farm at the turn of the century. In my day the bridge was used to provide a back entrance to Thorncliffe race track. Any Wednesday or Saturday in season, between 12:30 p.m. to 1:30 p.m. and 4:30 p.m. to 5:30 p.m., the loose planking of the bridge produced a sound like thunder as car after car rolled over it. These continuous claps of thunder caused our visitors to inquire if a storm was coming up. The race track public will remember that bridge well.

I was never a fisherman but had many friends who were ardent anglers. Dozens of boys could be seen along the Don on weekends trying a line in the river. The last salmon in the Don was seen in 1914. There was the sucker run in the period following the freshet when the water cleared. Hundreds of these large coarse fish could be easily caught then. Today there are no signs of suckers in the spring. But up until the Don Mills development the river sheltered brown trout, some carp, innumerable minnows and also one goldfish with a postage stamp stuck to its scales. This incredible fact was related to me by the man who caught the fish in front of my cottage. How a goldfish with a postage stamp could be found in the Don is open to conjecture. An upstream cottager may have attached the stamp and thrown the fish in the water as a lark. It sounds rather absurd but coming from Julian Hebert, the fisherman who caught it, I believed it.

CHAPTER SIXTEEN

Wells, Pumps and Water Witching

As I see it, the most important aspect of a place in the country is water. Water is all important, be it from a spring, a woodland pool, a brook, a river, lake or even in the form of rain pouring down a spout into a rain barrel.

There was water at the Forks of the Don but not on my acreage so I determined to locate it and dig a well. To do this I had recourse to the services of a "witcher", whose skill is otherwise known as water divining, water dowsing or water witching, a form of biological chemistry handed down to certain men and women since time immemorial.

My many experiences with witching have proven that it works: witchers do find water. In this the proof of the pudding is indeed in the eating. Digging for a well without first having located a source of water is something of a gamble.

The Metropolitan Toronto and Region Conservation Authority used witchers to locate all the wells in conservation areas. Lawrence Maltby, the Authority's expert on finding water, could almost smell it. He could simply look at a field and point to a water source. He found the splendid artesian spring that gushes out of the soil at Humber Trails.

While witching is practised primarily with a forked twig, metal devices, including a coat hanger, can also be used. Some of these devices swing like a pendulum in response to a hidden source of water or minerals.

Among my souvenirs of the outdoors is a forked branch which broke when Joe Allard, a witcher, tried to hold it rigid in his hands over a vein of water that he had located for me. In so doing the twig simply broke in his hand because of the unseen pressure on it. I kept it as a souvenir of the incredible for the incredulous.

When I took over the property at the Forks of the Don there was no working well or other source of drinking water available. There was a shaft of a sort back of the house and although I cleaned it out, only a trickle of water appeared at the bottom of this so-called well. Obviously, if I was going to have water, I would have to find it. For several years we made do, that is we used the Don water, which was quite clean in those days, for general purposes but brought out the drinking water from the city in jugs. This practice is still followed by many city people with summer cottages.

It was actually in 1935 before we seriously attempted to find water. One day my father said to me, "Frank Hill who inspects elevators for City Hall is a witcher. Frank will come out to the property in September to see if he can locate water for us." Now whatever you call it, witching, dowsing or water divining is as old or older than the Roman Empire. There is some speculation that Moses was acting as a witcher when he located the water that sprang from the rock. Witching means that some people have the power to locate water when they hold a forked twig in their hands. It cannot be just any kind of twig but should be of apple, cherry, hazel or willow wood. When the twig is held firmly by the two ends of its fork and the single end of the fork is bent downwards, it may be assumed that there is a vein of water at that point below the surface. Some people are sceptical about this but in my experience the chemical reaction in the body, or whatever makes a witcher, has been proven many times. The sources of water for large industrial plants have been located by witching.

On September 6, 1935 Frank Hill came out to the property as promised. "Water located in September means that there will be water all year round," he said. He thereupon took one forked twig from a collection of several, held the two ends in his hands and, with arms stretched forward, proceeded to pace the property from one end to the other. There was no response from the twig until he walked along our fence line at the base of the slope adjacent to the cottage property. Here suddenly the twig was pulled downwards by an unseen force. "It's a vein," Frank said as he followed it to the garden then across the garden to the driveway. He lost the vein there but then picked it up again. He explained that it was likely skirting a huge stone that had altered the water's course. However between the driveway and the river the presence of water seemed strong. Frank explained, "The flow starts at the top of the slope, works its way under the garden to eventually join the river. There is water here and lots of it at 15 to 17 feet. You are lucky. It's the only decent source I have found."

To convince us, Frank Hill tried to keep the twig rigid in his hands over the water course, whereupon the branch creaked and strained in its effort to respond to the call of the water. When he moved away from the vein to the right or to the left there was no response from the twig. Neither was there any response when Father or I held the twig in our hands. In these days, when so much has been explained, water divining still remains a mystery.

The next day, September 7, 1935, three of us commenced digging a shaft five feet by five feet. That afternoon we had dug down to the clay, at which point the subsoil turned to hard pan, which had to be chiselled out a piece at a time with a chisel and sledge hammer for a depth of about

114

ten feet. Meanwhile we had set up three poles over the shaft in wigwam fashion from which a pulley and rope were suspended. The pail was tied to the rope and lowered, filled with hard pan and pulled to the surface, then dumped near the shaft. We did this for several days.

By September 15 the shaft had been dug to a depth of 14 feet. Two days later a deposit of sharp, black sand was reached at a depth of 17 feet. Water began to ooze into the bottom of the shaft. At this point we encountered a large stone, which we dug out with some difficulty. Having removed this stone we poked a six-foot pole through the sand and met no resistance. Running water quickly filled the space left by the stone.

Quickly we bailed out the water several times to clear the bottom, then piled a quantity of small river stones in a circle on the floor of the well. Next we placed an oaken cask on top of the stones. Clay was then packed around the barrel up to its rim. By September 20 water had risen to a depth of four and a half feet in the cask. A second cask was placed on top of the first and it too was packed into the shaft with clay. Other casks were added to the shaft. The level of the water in the well never once dropped below eight feet, no matter how much we pumped, which indicated that the source was a running stream. Nor did the level drop during a rainless period of 40 days. As for the water, it was intensely cold, sulpherous at first, but sweet when this condition cleared up through use. The loss of that well was one I regretted most when my property was expropriated. I pleaded with the authorities to leave it for the use of people walking through the Valley, but the well was filled over.

After we had dug the well we built a suitable well top and installed an all-weather outdoor hand pump, which served us well during the years. It was the kind that lost its prime and required repriming with each use. It was a good feature as there was no possibility of it freezing up during the cold months.

The well had been in use several seasons when the following amusing incident (at least in retrospect it is amusing) occurred. I decided that the well water needed a treatment of lime, which I was told was the general practice. We had just moved back to the Valley for the summer. It was mid-May when I prepared to lime the water. I removed a board from the well cover, peeked down at the water in the oaken cask shaft and poured in a half pound or so of the lime. But this seemed such an insignificant amount that I simply poured in the entire five pound package.

Next morning I drew a glass of water from the kitchen pump. It was crystal clear. Success, I thought. It being Sunday we went to church and upon returning an hour or so later proceeded to have breakfast. Following this, water was boiled for the dishes and poured in a large basin with some soap added. This was no sooner done than the water turned to whitewash. My wife was furious when I explained how I thought the whitewash had originated. I was furious with myself when I realized that the consequences were going to be directed at me. There was no way that we could use the water. Greatly chagrined I called Frank Hill. "How much lime did you put in?" he asked. When I told him he said, "Wow! A half a pound would have been enough." "What will I do?" I asked. "Pump," he said. So pump I did, off and on until Wednesday, when the water cleared. It was a lesson about too much of a good thing.

In the spring of 1934 we had set up a kitchen pump and laid a line of 1½-inch pipe from the well to the kitchen, a distance of 160 feet up a slope. It was a positive joy to operate the pump handle and to watch the water flow abundantly from the spout, not worrying about how much water went down the sink.

This extravagance reminded me of a rather quaint arrangement during my early days at the Forks that was part of my continuing quest to do things the hard way.

The cottage stood on a river bank some 20 feet above the Don. We wanted to be able to pump water from the river instead of having to carry it. We also wanted some kind of a water system in the house itself. To facilitate this we built a platform halfway up the bank and laid a line of pipe from the river to a barrel set up on a couple of two by four planks in the rear corner of the house adjacent to the shed. The idea was to pump water from the river to the barrel. This could only be done with a hand pump by cutting down on pump lift via the platform, halfway up the bank. The barrel was provided with a pipe at the bottom, connected in turn to a tap over a sink in the corner of the living room. It was all very easy; water flowed from the taps providing the barrel was full. But filling the barrel was such hard work and we used water faster than we were willing to pump. After a few weeks we gave up the idea as impracticable. Actually it was one of the craziest innovations I had ever set my hand to.

Before the property was wired for electricity I bought what was called a chore horse, a gasoline-powered outfit made by the Johnson people in Peterborough. It was a tremendous little outfit that would provide electricity and pump water. It too was set on the platform halfway down the river bank. A whirl of the chore horse pedal and water poured out of the hose attached to it, as would have been the case in the city. Watering the lawns and the garden became a pleasure. The chore horse was one of the most satisfactory experiences of my 30 years at the Forks of the Don.

The chore horse prompted us to have the house wired. Having done this we had electric light, but only so long as the chore horse ran. So when guests came, on went the lights, and when they departed, the lights were switched off and we reverted to coal oil lamps.

Then, after living the life of 19th century pioneers for so many years, it was suddenly all over. I had travelled the route of battery radios, coal oil stoves, Aladdin lamps, hand-operated washing machines, everything that excluded the one final solution – electricity. The advantages of electricity over the simple life were so multiple that the simple life was laid

Photo shows method used to retain waters of spring before covering over, 1935.

quietly to rest for the most part. An electrician by the name of Taylor offered to run a line from Don Mills Road to the cottage, materials supplied, for $75, if we provided the poles, which we did. Eventually the line was buried underground.

Since time immemorial a spring trickled from out of a slope adjacent to the railway, about a quarter mile up Valley from my cottage. I was first aware of it in 1920, when my companions and I stopped there for a drink on our way to our camping place further up the Valley. It was a good spring with a taste of iron, so good that I felt that it should be preserved for future hikers. My friend, Eric La Trobe, and I set out to do this. First we started digging into the bank above the spring to cup the waters as they trickled down from the sides of this cut. The bottom of the area was then lined with stones. We then dug a second hole well below the first, into which we placed a small wooden cask. A piece of sheet metal in the form of a trough connected the cupped water with the rim of the cask. This conveyed the spring water to the cask, which then quickly filled.

We had previously bored a 1½-inch hole at the bottom of the cask into which we inserted a three-foot length of pipe through which the water in the cask flowed. When these preparations had been completed we covered the excavation and cask with sheet metal, rocks and sod. The camouflage was almost perfect. All that could be seen was the tip of the pipe, from which poured a gentle flow of water. It was all very "spring-

117

like". To round out matters we placed a flat stone below this pipe on which the water fell with a tinkling sound. A few cans and a cup were placed nearby for passers-by. Henceforth, we agreed, anyone wanting a cold drink would be assured of one. We were quite pleased with ourselves and thought that the flow would continue forever.

The spring lasted for one season. Unbelievably one of those oafs with whom society is afflicted tried to pry the pipe loose. He must have tried very hard for he twisted it to the point where it lost the water's flow. He never did pry the pipe loose. So once again the waters of the spring were dispersed, lost in the soil and deflected from the use we had intended. However, our primitive engineering still remains beneath its camouflage and will likely remain so until kingdom come.

CHAPTER SEVENTEEN

Wood and What Went With It

We used a lot of wood in my day. There was always an abundance of firewood lying around. The driftwood that lined the river's shores or which became lodged in our small dam provided a constant supply. The adjoining slope of the Valley at the Forks were littered with dead and broken branches, more than we could ever use. These were usually gathered in winter and hauled across the river ice with a sleigh.

We always needed wood because in the '30s wood stoves were very much in use and sold at prices low compared to those of wood stoves today. Many of them were available through second-hand stores. My cottage was heated with wood, likewise our kitchen at home. When I married I made fires of wood in the furnace during the early fall and late spring. Then there were the outdoor fires and the indoor fireplace, all of which required wood. Finally there was the 30-gallon evaporator-boiler which we used for heating water, and this too required wood.

However wood must be sawed into suitable lengths, which means work, a lot of work. But it was not all drudgery. We purposely piled the driftwood, including many logs, and left this flotsam to dry until late August. During the winter we held sawing bees, using a two-man cross-cut saw on these occasions. Today it would be more convenient to own a chain-saw. But something can be said for the joy of feeling the blood race throughout one's body on a moonlit winter evening, to the steady cadence of the "zing, zing, zing", as two robust men moved the cross-cut saw back and forth through a cut of maple.

The most unique use of wood I made up the Don was to saw a seven-foot length from a dead white pine tree. The bark when removed revealed the tiny tunnels chiselled by beetles a generation before. Eventually the log was placed over the mantle of the downstairs fireplace on Hillside Drive. It is still there, aged with time and the making of many fires, a reminder of the tree's lifespan, or part of it.

I had a great deal of experience with wood during my stay at the Forks of the Don. I had a deep friendly feeling for wood, associating it with the warmth and comfort by a fireside. I also knew the effort required to collect sufficient wood for our needs.

Living by the Don River brought me in close contact with wood, particularly in the winter when I drew my Indian sleigh over the ice to fetch load after load of dead branches. In the spring the freshets brought down a continuous supply of tree trunks, logs, branches and other debris that could be used for fuel. I fished this flotsam from the flood waters with a 15-foot pike pole and became very skilled at this. Wood thus salvaged was left in a pile to dry during the summer, to be sawed up during the fall for winter use.

The Indian sleigh was sold to me by Mr. George, the railway section foreman, for $1.00. It was sturdy and stood on eight-inch posts fastened to steel runners which were three inches wide. It was constructed of strips of wood three inches wide. The sleigh was designed to travel over light snow and was especially suited for drawing heavy loads over the ice. When it was loaded, I could pull the sleigh with one finger, it ran so smoothly. I used it on Saturday mornings when I pulled it upstream to places where pieces of dead wood could be picked up or where cedars uprooted by storms could be sawed into fence post lengths.

I was not the only one looking for firewood. A fellow by the name of Steve Debnarik, who stayed for a while in the de Grassi cottage, used a model T Ford truck to travel over the ice to bring down loads of firewood. I have a picture of this.

Gathering wood was a tradition on my place. It required a healthy attitude toward the job ahead, good arm and leg muscles, a sharp cross-cut saw, an assortment of wedges, a mallet and a sharp axe, plus the time to indulge in the pastime.

Using a cross-cut saw required some skill. It was a pleasure or a chore depending who used the saw. The trick was to pull on the blade then let go so the other fellow could pull away easily from you. This established a rhythmic motion that made light work of sawing through a tree trunk. Tugging on the saw made it difficult to handle.

The wood we picked up along the Don was mostly elm, oak, ash, cedar, pine, maple, beech, birch and hemlock, to name a few. I got to know each kind of wood by its texture and fragrance, especially hemlock and apple. A few pieces of apple wood in the woodshed perfumed it like a barrel of apples.

Wood must be dry to burn properly and there has to be starting wood or kindling to start the fire. That meant a woodshed which, like a good bank account, guaranteed security against a rainy day or a cold night. It also reflected the measure of one's forethought and husbandry. Usually I had a stock of wood several years in advance of the need for it. My woodshed often became an oasis where I rummaged for wood, sometimes to the sound of the rain pattering on the roof, amid the fragrant scents from the hemlock, cherry or apple wood.

As I was often alone I had to use a one-man cross-cut saw or a Swedish saw that I still use today. It is as sharp as a razor. Chain-saws were

Steve Debnarik, handyman with his saw equipment, de Grassi lot, 1935.

unknown in those days. Sawing wood was a therapy of a sort. I still saw wood to rid myself of whatever concerns I may have. Like I have found that chopping wood simply dissolves whatever anger or frustration may have taken hold of me. If only for these reasons working with wood has a price beyond measure.

In the 1980s wood stoves are very much in the limelight. I recollect that in the 1930s the Trows had a wood-burning kitchen stove made in Manitoba. It had been made especially for western Canadian conditions and was fueled by small poplar branches that would burn in it for hours.

Over the years I used several wood stoves, mostly the box type. The veteran of these stoves, which I still use, could hold a dozen good sized cuts of elm or any other wood. It was constructed to draw cold air from the floor and disperse the warm air throughout the room. The stove could be filled with wood in the evening and would burn all night. That stove could heat my cottage up the Don in a matter of minutes. Even today a few handfulls of chips and wood sweepings in that same stove suffice to warm up my workshop.

In my early days along the Don, the river Flats were dotted with huge majestic old elms, especially near the Forks of the Don. They were our pride and joy, a viewpoint that will be shared by thousands of Canadians who were familiar with this spectacle. We never thought at the time that they would someday be wiped out. But they were and sadly I saw the top branches die in tree after tree until the Dutch elm disease disposed of

121

them all. The disease became so widespread that the province of Ontario and the municipalities organized work crews to saw the trees down. It was sad indeed to lose these elms which cast their shade in summer and from the tips of whose branches the orioles suspended their nests.

On one occasion at the turn of the year a crew passed through the area, sawing elms on the Flats across from the de Grassi cottage. I soon became aware of 14 huge slices of elm that had been left in the wake of the work crew. These cuts were oblong in shape, about five feet long and three feet across and eight inches thick. I organized a crew of my own, got out the Indian sleigh and had all 14 cuts skidded across the ice to my wood yard. The cuts, by the way, could be picked up without asking. My son-in-law made two magnificent coffee tables with two of the cuts, one of which I still have. The other cuts were given away for the same purpose. My coffee table top draws admiring comments from all my guests when they see the table for the first time.

I am a keen collector of mementos of the past. The pine log which straddles my fireplace was cut from a dead tree on the slope back of the cottage. Several of these pine trees that died in the '20s are still standing on that slope, immersed in new growth. One day, in a poetic mood, I wrote a poem to that old pine log. It was something about us both travelling through life together, although obviously the pine had had a head start.

The white elm seems to be coming back. I see the young trees everywhere, many of which have already attained a height of 30 to 40 or more feet. Time will tell. In the Tweed area, white elm is still a predominant part of the pastoral scene.

Before the Dutch elm disease got underway, wind and erosion had toppled several of the giants on the Flats where Taylor Creek enters the East Don. These were no ordinary trees. They had trunks that two men with arms outstretched could not have spanned and their tentacular branches were proportionately huge. This bounty attracted M. Amede Hamel who, as a country man, could not stand to see this wood wasted. So along with a few helpers he proceeded to saw and split all of the wood he needed. He got two truck loads, enough for the winter. Acting on my urgings, Hamel had sense enough to have the wood promptly removed to his home on Broadview Avenue where it was safe and secure. As I had learned, a branch or a log may lie on the ground untouched for a long while, but wood sawed up into stove-length pieces is a different matter.

It was late August and the Labour Day weekend was in the offing. The word about the wood had got round among the men in the CNR Leaside shops. Several of Hamel's workmates thought they too would like to have some of this wood. There was one chap, whose name I do not recall, who masterminded the operation, with Joe Giguere and others helping. They had a tough assignment. What was left of the toppled elms was largely butt ends and huge trunks. However they sawed and split the wood and had one picnic to ease the work along. They finished a few days before Labour Day. What had been a fortress of elm trunks was now stacked-up stove wood, five feet high to a length of about 40 feet. A tempting array to say the least.

The sight of all that sawed wood made me apprehensive. I urged the men repeatedly to get it out of the Valley fast. But they wanted to go home to Quebec for the holiday weekend and said the wood could wait until they got back. They would have it out of there by Tuesday. I shook my head in dismay but I could not prevail upon them to change their minds. They were adamant; the wood could wait until Tuesday.

On the Saturday night of the Labour Day weekend, 1943, the wood disappeared, every last stick of it. I had strong suspicions as to who took it. Tell-tale marks of large truck tires led from the wood pile to the ascent cut into the Valley slope and from there to the top of the Valley near what is now Parkview Hills. Someone had "figgered" the wood was his and that was all there was to it.

When the men returned on Tuesday with a truck for the wood they found that the bird had flown. They had worked in their spare time for weeks for nothing. It was a mean trick but as I have learned, the path of life is generously strewn with mean tricks. That was the end of communal wood sawing at the Forks of the Don.

My father often told a story about a theft of wood in his village of Williamstown in Glengarry County, Ontario. A neighbour noticed that his wood pile was becoming depleted but could never catch anyone taking the wood. He made plans to find out who it was. He took several pieces of kindling, bored a hole in each with an auger, put some gunpowder in each hole and sealed it with a wooden plug. A few mornings later, just about dawn, an explosion was heard coming from a farmhouse down the road. It was noted later that the front of the kitchen stove had blown out. The charge was strong enough to do its work but not to injure anyone. My father's neighbour never complained about losing wood after that.

I too have suffered through tampering with my wood pile. After Father closed down the poultry operation, I stockpiled kindling in the coops, stacking it in rows against the back walls. Whenever I looked at the stock everything seemed normal. However when I began to draw on the supply late in the winter, I discovered that when the top layers were removed the whole structure collapsed. What should have been solid rows of stacked stove wood had become a hollow shell. It was a poor camouflage for the theft of my kindling. There really is no defence against this sort of thing. It is just a matter of biding one's time and removing the cause of the nuisance. I am consoled by the fact that for every dubious character I have met, there are a dozen men I would trust implicitly.

Thoreau wrote that his wood warmed him twice, when he cut it and when he burned it. I can add that in addition to these two attributes, my wood has survived in memory all these 50 years or more to warm the cockles of my heart in the remembrance of the hundreds of fires I have enjoyed. Pine roots and pine knots were my favourite fuel. The roots were present everywhere on the Valley slopes, where they were reminders of the pine forests that once stood there. These roots could be easily pulled from the soil and it required little effort to gather a quantity of them. Being resinous they never rotted and kept forever the rosy tints of their wood. The roots burned fiercely and exuded a fragrance not unlike the perfume of carnations. No wood ever surpassed their flames for sheer beauty or the art of their fiery caves or caverns among the glowing embers. It was a pity to ever burn them for they could, in the hands of an artisan, become ornaments of beauty.

Pine knots were harder to come by. There were a few around on the Valley slopes but mostly they came with pine slash from saw mill operations. It was from this last source that I once obtained a large supply of pine knots. In the thirties we often visited friends who had built a cottage in the Pickering pine glades directly west of the present Greenwood conservation area. It so happened that during one of these visits I became aware of a large pile of pine slash from a saw mill operation. Slash is actually the outer surface of the bark of the pine tree and the butt end of the knots. It was a real find and the knots were free for the taking. That afternoon we filled two large jute bags with the biggest knots I could find.

In those days I had an outdoor fireplace with a comfortable seat. Usually I made my fires at dusk and sat there until close to midnight when the last of the evening trains to Ottawa and Montreal were on their way. I could hear these trains pulling into and leaving the Leaside Station. It was a sound I liked to listen to. I had planned to feed the knots into my fires for the rest of the summer and left the jute bags close to the fire pit – too close as it turned out.

As usual I slept on a cot on the veranda. I awakened at 2:00 a.m. to the pleasing scent of burning pine. The odour carried me on a vaporous carpet of pleasant dreams until suddenly I sat bolt upright, sniffing the air for confirmation of a fear that had suddenly entered my mind. I glanced toward the fireplace where a magnificent blaze was in full progress. The jute bags had caught fire and the knots were burning with abandon. They were so far gone that there was nothing to do but to let the fire burn itself out. I never gathered so many knots again at one time.

Some wood was easy to come by but you had to watch for it. Used railway ties, or sleepers as they were called, were stacked along the right-of-way and burned by the section gang at regular intervals. These could be had for the asking. What a price they would fetch today for patio and garden purposes! But being full of tar and gravel, they could foul up a stove and play havoc with the edge of an axe. While splitting one of these blocks a pebble struck me in the left eye, the effect of which were felt for some months afterwards.

Arnold Tucker sitting on a pile of Hemlock boards. Last wood to be milled from Taylor Creek park about 1935.

Back in the thirties Don Mills Road spanned the CNR line at de Grassi Hill with a wooden trestle bridge. The floor of the bridge, all loose B.C. fir beams about 16 feet long by two feet wide and eight inches thick, made a racket like thunder every time a car passed over them. The wear on this planking was such that the floor of the bridge had to be renewed every few years.

I noticed one fall evening that 32 of these beams or planks had been piled up beside the railway bank across the Don from my cottage. Mr. George, the section foreman, told me that he had been ordered to burn them by Wednesday. "Could you leave them for a few days more?" I inquired. "I think I can get them out of here." He agreed. I called Joe Giguere to give me a hand and we proceeded to salvage the timber.

My equipment included a set of "dogs". This tool consisted of a two-man handle with a set of pointed, free-moving grippers suspended from the middle of the handle. The grippers, when pressed into the wood, tightened automatically as soon as the log or timber was carried by the dogs. The leverage made it possible for two men to drag a heavy piece of timber which otherwise would have been beyond their strength. It was exactly the tool needed for the salvage job. For several evenings we went to the pile and placed the dogs dead centre of each timber so that it balanced evenly when we carried it over the track. At the river bank we gave each timber a heave-ho, which toppled them down the bank to the

125

Hauling wood down the Don. Model T version, 1935.

river shore. In this way we rescued all 32 of the timbers, which remained in a pile until the freeze up. It was then an easy matter to "snake" or push them over the ice to my side of the river, where they were hauled for safety. For two men it had been quite a feat of arms, or rather of dogs. In due course I used the wood mostly for kindling but I have thought many times how some fellow trying to build a house would have been glad to have had those timbers.

Metropolitan Toronto Parks Department follows the practice of dumping sawed wood from pruning and thinning operations in piles in the parks for public use. On other occasions municipalities have hauled entire truck loads of firewood to the dump. I was walking through Taylor's Bush one day when I noticed a huge pile of branches, sawed tree trunks and cuts of wood obviously waiting to be removed. I made inquiries. Yes, the wood was going to the dump. "Well," I said, "as I am just around the corner, would you drop it off there?" They agreed. So I met the chap who did the hauling and sure enough the wood was dumped at the rear of the de Grassi property. There remained in the truck about 40 pieces of maple sawed from tree trunks. "You would not want those, would you?" he asked. "I sure would. I'll take them," I replied. It took me the winter, off and on, to dispose of the pile. The maple cuts split beautifully.

Fifty years ago I prided myself on being rather handy with an axe. To some extent I still am. One Sunday morning many years ago I took my two daughters, aged ten and eight years, to Trow Hill. There was a pile of red oak blocks outside the house. I asked Mrs. Trow if she would mind if I split a few for the exercise. She smiled at this and handed me the axe. I brought it down on a block of red oak with all of my strength. But it rebounded as though it had struck a block of rubber. I tried again and again but after 20 minutes had only managed to chip off two pieces. The wood was like iron.

The blocks may have been easier to handle when full of frost. Today there is an axe on the market with built-up sides that splits the wood quite easily. There was nothing like that around at the time of my wood-splitting days.

CHAPTER EIGHTEEN

Cabins

To boys in my day there was magic in the thought of building a log cabin in the woods. Hundreds of Toronto boys held the dream of making one ever since Ernest Thompson Seton wrote his famous story about Yan and his cabin in Mud Creek ravine.

It seems certain that at one time or another dozens of log cabins were built up the Don and in adjacent ravines. A fine cabin was made of logs by boys of the 45th troop in the Warden woods during the winter of 1922-23 and in which I had a part.

All cabins eventually suffered the same fate; they simply disappeared. Some were well made while others were a mere collection of driftwood. Sometimes fine trees were hacked in the process of building these cabins.

These cabins pointed to a need that gripped the imagination of the boys of my day. To them the Don Valley was an escape and to have one's cabin there was a sheer joy. I know the experience of stepping out of a well-made cabin within a few feet of a creek and feeling that I was a hundred miles from the city.

Today building a cabin in the woods of the Don is no longer a realizeable dream for boys. The woods are silent now and seem to be growing back more thickly than in generations past, free as they are of cattle, grass fires and the boys who had set out to build their own cabins.

Walk, ramble or hike, it all added up to footsteps. While writing my history of the Don Valley I hiked by stages along the entire length of the East and West Valleys of the Don to the very headwaters of the streams that eventually came together to form the Don River. The east branch rose in a thicket of cedar on the Elgin Mills sideroad owned then by E. McConnell, who had persuaded his father not to chop down the cedars. Tiny springs and rivulets in this wetland quickly formed a brook which, as it widened, became the East Don. The west branch rose from a single spring within view of the hamlet of Teston, once known as Thamesville.

In my day, and I suppose it happened many times before, individuals who were attracted to the Don Valley tried to establish themselves on a more permanent basis and built cabins. Ed Else, a one-time scoutmaster

Cabin on author's property was built by Ed Else a former Scout master. From right, Arnold Tucker, the author and Ed Else. Photo 1938.

and a veteran of the First World War, got my permission to build a cabin on land I owned across from my cottage. It was a well-built cabin. Ed used railway ties for the walls and filled the cracks with clay. He used the cabin on a year-round basis and I have some excellent pictures of it. Ed also made a garden, a small tennis court and a swimming hole in the Don. He was a good neighbour and we liked to have him around.

The fellow we called Carl the Dane, although there was some question if indeed he was a Dane, was something else. He just moved in, squatted no less, and built a rather spacious cabin up the East Don Valley on a slope overlooking the first railway bridge, a quarter mile up Valley from my cottage. Carl did not welcome visitors and when called on was visibly anxious to curtail the visit. He kept a goat and eventually moved out.

We never knew who actually owned much of the land in the Valley. There were no signs to warn people against trespassing, except in a few cases, so a fellow like Carl could just move in and take things for granted.

The 32 acres that the CNR had offered me were purchased by a fellow who I will not name. He and his father made a market garden of a sort near the frog pond. They spent as much time quarrelling with each other as they did working. One day I heard chopping from the top of a railway cut up Valley and went to investigate. Chopping always meant damage to trees in some form. There was our friend, busy chopping down white pine trees to make a cabin. It was his land but I felt like throw-

129

ing him off it. "Why," I asked, "are you destroying your scenery and the environment to make this? It's not even a good cabin. In six months from now you won't use it and the trees will be gone." I was right. The duo sold the land and the cabin was soon pulled apart by the youth of the day. All that remained were the stumps of the trees which, had they been left alone, would be full grown.

"Tex", "Flea" and "Deacon" were a strange trio indeed. Tex came from a good family and had a propensity for playing Indian. Flea was a young man who liked the outdoor life. Deacon was a very large tame crow who participated in telling the fortunes of the boys who swam in Clay Banks swimming hole. Tex and Flea made a wigwam in a pine grove near the swimming hole. Tex was a painter of oils of considerable merit and a well-dressed man. I am not sure if it was Tex or Flea who carved in wood but I have several scenes from the Valley carved in wood which I bought from them many years ago. Deacon the crow was something of a black villain who I did not trust too much, particularly when small children were around. As crows are attracted to bright objects, I always kept an eye on him when the trio came to visit us.

Eventually the trio left the Valley and set up a "trading post" closer to North Bay than to Toronto. Some of the readers of this story may remember an incident that was recorded in the newspapers at the time. Tex was dressed in Indian garb and on an American tourist's request did a war dance while the tourist took movies of him. Tex pointed the rifle he was carrying at the tourist at his request. Then, as the tourist was taking more movies, Tex pulled the trigger and shot the tourist dead. It was a horrible accident and attributable to the fact that Tex had no idea whatsoever that the rifle was loaded.

Boys of my day frequently built cabins in the woods, but they were usually so poorly built and devastated the surrounding woodlands to such an extent that I will refrain from further comment. Some of the finest stands of cedar, hemlock and white pine were hacked away by thoughtless youth. It is only today that these species are creeping back in the Valley.

In the '20s and '30s several scout troops and other groups of young men set up some very good camps in the Valley, usually for the summer. The finest of these was on a flat bordering the river a short distance up Valley from my cottage. About 12 young men had pooled resources. They had several tents, including a cook tent, and employed a man to look after the camp and do their cooking. These young men all worked. They pedalled their bikes into the city for the day and returned to the camp after work. The flat was large enough for a baseball diamond and I am sure that the fellows had a good time. Most certainly they were clever enough to see that they could enjoy all the pleasures of a camp right at the city's door.

I had a Don Valley cabin of my own, situated a few yards from our kitchen. It was expertly built of cedar logs I purchased from a man by the

Wigwam camp of Tex and Flea, 1934.

name of Babcock, who had done some thinning in a woodlands north of Mount Albert. The logs with the bark removed were laid upright then varnished. This was my retreat. It was furnished with a desk, a few chairs and a couch. I spent many happy hours there writing, looking out of windows that gave an excellent view of the Valley. The cabin was demolished when my property was expropriated for the Don Valley Parkway. I carried the cedar logs, one or two at a time, across my cable bridge to the de Grassi property. Here they were stockpiled and put to various uses.

In the 1970s a group of boys or young men, who called themselves the Huckleberry Hutters, built a cabin on the crest of the Valley on what was once known as Milne's Hollow. I never met them, although they used the cabin for several years. The cabin was well made and spacious and commanded a lofty view of the Don. As for the group's name, I never heard of huckleberries growing in the Don Valley .

Ed Else was also thinking of something foreign to the Valley when he named his property "Sunova-beach". This name was lettered in painted river stones and set in a mound of soil in the railway track in full view of hikers.

Else told me that on a Sunday morning a man stopped on the track to look at the lettering. He kept saying the words out loud and finally the twist that he was looking for came to him. He burst out laughing, repeating "Sunova Beach, Sunova Beach" and "Sunova something else". Else thought the incident was rather amusing.

The idea of building a cabin in the woods is far from the average boy's thoughts today. So why was it so attractive to so many boys who frequented the Valley in the '20s and '30s?

In those days we were still within recent memory of the generations who had cleared the land and lived in log cabins while working towards better times. Furthermore the early movies often featured scenarios of backwoods settlements being attacked by Indians and the besieged defending themselves in cabins. And back in the '20s boys were often thrown on their own resources, with a lot of time on their hands and little money in their pockets. To them building a cabin had its allure. It was the excitement of being able to get away from parental discipline and to run free in the woods with a shelter of their own that captured their imaginations.

CHAPTER NINETEEN

How to Lose a Fortune

This chapter underlines the ease with which fortunes could be made in the '30s by buying land at bargain prices and reselling later at top prices. Being in the right place at the right time describes it.

Everyone had the opportunity to be involved in some measure with land speculation but not everyone had the wisdom or the means of making these profitable decisions. As in everything, decisions were made within the context of the times and each person's financial position. Few of us could foresee the unbelievable rise in land prices that would follow the Second World War.

I was personally more interested in preserving greenbelt land than in trying to make money in land. Ventures in real estate did not occur to me. Undoubtedly it would have been a rewarding experience to have become a very wealthy man. On the other hand the road to riches is not necessarily lined only with dollars. To be able to recall many events of the past is a form of wealth in itself. To have had the health to survive them is wealth at its most meaningful.

My father, who came to Toronto in 1882 to work on the dredging of the Don River, was offered a long strip of property on Broadview Avenue between Queen and what was later Danforth Avenue. "Take it if only for the taxes," the owner said, but my father passed up the offer. A generation later I was offered parcels of land which, had I acted decisively, would have made me in the ensuing years a very rich man. But in this nostalgia of hindsight I am not alone. Hundreds of native Torontonians could tell similar stories. Land prices in those days were absolutely nothing compared with today, but the same was true of earnings.

To give some idea of how things were, I rented my cottage on the Don from Canadian National Railways for $5.00 a month and bought it for $300. Eventually I bought four acres of land from CNR and the de Grassi cottage for $1,000.

In those days the Railway owned several tracts of land along the Valley and at one point proposed to sell them. One of these tracts was a 32-acre parcel of Valley, slope, Valley bottom land and acreage on the edge of the Valley. The Railway real estate department offered to sell me this

Fireplace of Billy McLean's residence. Railway in distant background where Grand and Toy and other plants are located today. McLean would take train after leaving Toronto World (later Globe and Mail) office. Train engineers made a special stop for him across from his house. Photo 1936.

property for $3,000, payable, if I wished, over a period of 15 years. I was lukewarm about the offer, as I felt that I owned enough property at the time, and was otherwise dissuaded from making the purchase. The property went through several owners and, to complete my story quickly, eventually an apartment building was put up. I was told in the '60s by an architect that the four acres on which that apartment building stood, which were just part of the 32 acres I had been offered, were worth $750,000.

In the '30s an alert, knowledgeable person could have picked up a lot of property. My father and I drove along Don Mills Road one evening in response to an advertisement about a lot which was for sale for $2,000. The lot, incidentally, was located on the southeast corner of Lawrence Avenue and what was then Don Mills Road. It was about 200 feet wide and perhaps 600 feet deep. I could never understand why my father, who had managed to own four houses in his lifetime while earning $30 a week, could have turned his back on the $2,000 lot with the remark, "Who wants land so far out in the country?"!

Well, the story of that lot was like many others. A man by the name of Le Gris from Winnipeg bought it and at one point the B.P. Company bought the corner of the lot for a service station and paid $175,000. That was quite a number of years ago. As for the rest of the lot, now filled with

134

apartment buildings, like the young man in the Bible, I turn my head sadly away every time I pass there. But do I really? In the '30s my salary was $75 a week. I had a family to raise and a Depression to face. I also lived with the belief that times would get worse. There were too many despondent people around and some actually committed suicide. It was as bad as that.

Nevertheless some of my friends who were much smarter than I did very well. Rand Freeland bought an old run-down brick house on Pottery road for $500 and built it up to the successful Fantasy Farm of today. Rand could smell a land deal and he made some good ones. He came to me and said, "Charles, buy the northeast corner of John and Yonge Streets. It's for sale." I was experiencing at the time an upheaval in my business affairs and had the family to consider. I could not risk the $75,000, or rather I did not have the confidence to do so. Within a few months the lot was sold to a food chain for $250,000.

When Hillside Drive South was opened, a man by the name of Workman operated a temporary one-room real estate office on Broadview Avenue. He was selling ravine lots at $1,000 apiece. I bought one and could have had several. But I was obsessed at the time with paying insurance policies to ensure the education of my children. Today a vacant lot on Hillside Drive South, if such a lot existed, would be worth a lot of money. This sort of thing could go on endlessly. Nealon Taylor offered me the old family mansion that stood on the corner of Old Pottery Road and Broadview Avenue for $13,000.

A neighbour, who did very well when a company he had helped to build up was sold, said to me one day, "I would have thought that with all the conservation work, you would have made a million dollars for yourself by now." I can answer that by stating that while with the Metropolitan Toronto and Region Conservation Authority I contributed to every facet of the preservation of the Metropolitan Toronto greenbelt system. Authority-owned land during my tenure in office increased from a few hundred acres of parkland to 25,000 acres. Through the Nature Conservancy of Canada I have been involved with 252 individual property purchases of natural area land and that is only part of the story.

In truth I am far from being alone in the class of men who place a particular challenge or belief before their personal gain. It happens every day. In my case the challenge was the preservation of the greenbelt. While there may have been opportunities for gain, it never occurred to me to take advantage of them. I would no more have thought of turning over a few fast bucks for myself while entrusted with buying greenbelt land than I would have considered jumping off the Bloor Street viaduct.

There has been a substantial reward in this. My reward lay in the satisfaction of bringing to fruition a dream I had cherished for a long while. This reward is visible every time I walk over land that I have helped to secure for the public good. There are many scales on which to weigh the

Lawrence Avenue and Don Mills Road about 1938. School house was on the north-east corner. The Elm trees on the south-east corner. This lot was for sale in 1935 or thereabouts for $2,000.00. The Elm corner was sold for $225,000.00 to B.P. Petroleum. Background is of woodlands adjoining Don Valley.

value of a fortune and many ways to consider just what constitutes a fortune. I will leave it at that.

Some people were propelled by accident or the fortunes of life into entering into favourable property circumstances. For example, a number of the men who kept pigs in the Don Valley were forced to move out when pig raising was prohibited by law in East York. Several of them moved to Wexford and acquired farm land there in advance of the building boom.

People often sold out at what seemed fantastic prices, only to learn later that they should not have sold their property at the time. "Why I could have got ten times as much." Some of us are imbued with a different set of values. To each his own.

CHAPTER TWENTY

A Few Floral Friends

At some future date the Don and other Toronto region valleys will be carpeted once more with wild flowers as they were as recently as the 1920s.

Trillium, hepatica, bloodroot, wild phlox and other species are no longer seen in their onetime abundance because they were over picked. However these species and others, if left alone, will gradually make their way back. In some areas this is already taking place. The trillium is now Ontario's provincial or emblem flower. It should be growing in abundance in every woodland near and far from the large centres of population.

No woodland can convey that extra dimension of natural charm unless wild flowers are present. Without them woodlands are merely a collection of trees. With them our woodlands become a constant source of botanical values that make them a reservoir of flowering plants which are indeed part of our natural heritage.

One day, in the early thirties, I was walking down Yonge Street below King Street when I was attracted to a window display of a pocket-size book printed in brown ink and profusely illustrated with pictures of eastern Canadian wild flowers. The author, Magistrate Edmund Jones, obviously loved his subject and had cleverly featured as many as ten flowers per page, grouping them as to colour and season. I entered the store and bought a copy of the book for $1.00.

That spring the book was my constant outdoor companion and inspired me to identify one by one the flowers which I had so often seen but could not name. The book was exactly what I needed for in those days the Don Valley and its side ravines were vast storehouses of wild flowers, most of which were unknown to me. That little book, which I inadvertently lost, served me well. However, having a book as a guide was one thing. Finding examples of all the flowers in the book was quite another. Some species did not grow extensively in the Valley. For example, there was only one place in the Don Valley where I ever found the fringed gentian, and this only through naturalist Hugh Halliday, who had found it before me. Likewise the yellow lady's slipper, which I found only on a spring-fed slope and wetland back of my cottage. I never did find the showy lady's slipper, but it undoubtedly grew at one time in the Don Valley.

It was amazing what so small a book could do for a person. Flowers I previously passed by with a shrug and "I really don't know what it is" could now be identified. This little book opened a new avenue of knowledge to me. These discoveries added greatly to the pleasure of my field tours from spring to fall.

The very first floral arrival to greet spring was undoubtedly the skunk cabbage, which with some stretch of the imagination could be called a wild flower. Purple hoods or spathes, the size of half a cob of corn, pushed through the ice and snow in mid-March. I have seen this phenomena along the base of the Valley slope on which Chesterhill Road abuts. The slope was dotted with springs and seemed to be an ideal place for skunk cabbage. It smells like its name suggests, emitting an odour which under other circumstances would have turned me away. But to go to that little pocket of nature on a late March evening, when the days are noticeably longer, and to see those spathes pushing out of the snow, was a balm for the soul. The odour was the sweet scent of spring. By just being there the skunk cabbages added their twopence to the ode of spring, very much like the raspy call of a crow heard on the same hillside at the same time.

In the '20s and '30s entire slopes of the East Don Valley, from the Forks of the Don to Lawrence Avenue, were carpeted with flowering trilliums in the spring. It was an unforgettable sight and would be with us today had the trillium not been ruthlessly picked by uninformed people. The trillium reproduces through seeding and multiplication of flower stalks. The flower appears on a single stalk which also holds three leaves, so when the flower is picked, the leaves are also removed from the plant. this sets it back very badly. Actually it takes two or three years before the plant flowers again. If it is picked once more after this it may never recover.

It disturbed me to see each spring young people walking down the railway track with great bunches of triliium which they often threw away on the way home as the flowers and leaves become limp shortly after picking. Inevitably the trillium all but disappeared from the Valley and it is only now, 50 years later, that the plant is beginning to recover. Fortunately children today are educated in the principles of conservation and know that trillium should not be picked.

The trillium's normal growth pattern provides for a new stalk or several of them each year, along with seeds that become seedlings. Eventually a clump of trillium may contain 30 or 40 flowering stalks and be surrounded with innumerable seedlings. This is why hillsides do become veritable carpets of trillium.

The most profuse stands of white trillium with the largest flowers were on the slopes adjacent to Donlands Farm and the woods of the MacLean's sugar bush. Apart from the trillium there were so many wild flower species growing in this area that I called it wild flower paradise. Alas, since then paradise has fallen. There remains only thinned-out trees, grassed-over flood plain and nearby apartment buildings. But in my day it was something else. To the Don Valley Hiking Club, which held an annual tryst with the Donlands Farm trilliums, perhaps it was an ode to spring, or a festival of May, or perhaps just a ramble during which 40 people or more walked the hog's backs to the river bank where the festival was held. The ceremony included a huge pot of coffee which was often enough enriched with cream that Mrs. Murdock MacKenzie of Donlands Farm provided when we passed through. This sort of thing enlivens the jaded soul and even now is rich in memories that never fade. Well, there is no use crying over spilled milk, or cream as the case may be. Donlands Farm is gone, the sugar bush has been cleaned out save for a few skeletal trees and the trilliums have largely disappeared.

However, a floral species, if left alone, will regenerate itself. Years ago I thought I could help nature by making a wild flower garden among my own trees, which I did with some success. I brought in large quantities of pine needles, then made paths and transplanted many of the common species just to preserve them. I once experimented with a clump of showy lady's slipper I had brought in from another area. I do not counsel anyone to do this. I worked out an elaborate system of subterranean conduits fed from a central water system to duplicate natural conditions but the orchids eventually died. I am glad that I limited the experiment to one clump, as I am loath to interfere with natural wild flower growth.

Cattle and hogs, both of which roamed freely in the Valley in the '20s and '30s, were also a factor in the depletion of wild flower species. But they are gone and many a woodlot through which cattle once roamed 40 and more years ago is returning to a natural state. Nothing so elates me as to see in a restored woodlot nature edging back through wild flower species which I felt had disappeared forever in that location, or to see little groves of spruce and balsam spring up. Perhaps we of the D.V.C.A. made some contribution through our campaigns with slogans such as "Yours to enjoy, not to destroy" and the borrowed slogan "Take nothing but pictures, leave nothing but footsteps."

There were flowers other than the trillium for which we waited eagerly. The first true floral herald of spring was the hepatica, and it was often in a race with the mayflower and the bloodroot for the honour. We had splendid stands of hepaticas in the Don Valley and spur ravines. Probably the most extensive was in the woodlands that disappeared when the Leslie Street extension was built, just north of the Inn on the Park. It was a joy to see these woodlands suddenly vibrant with the pastel tints of lavender, mauve, white, pink and blue hepatica flowers. I called this place Hepatica Hillside, took some excellent pictures of it and wrote a few verses to its memory which lie buried somewhere in my notes.

To me the hepatica always seemed to be a direct link with spring, even in the depths of winter. At times during my hikes, with a group who could benefit from the lesson, I looked for the thick evergreen leaves of the hepatica. When the snow was brushed from the leaves, the central floral spikes were revealed. I would then take one of these spikes and cut it in two with a sharp knife. There in embryo were pistils and petals in their dormant stage, ready for the warming days of spring. There was something miraculous about a process that could make a flower that would grace a hillside the following spring. If ever I needed a lesson in hope it would be through nature's perpetuation of the hepatica.

I was fortunate to have Don Valley companions with a special interest in wild flowers who pooled resources with me. These included Arnold Tucker, who took hundreds of pictures of our favourite stands of wild flowers, from the may apple of early May to the swamp aster of September. Likewise Fletcher Sharp, who mounted specimens of wild flowers in huge scrap-books for educational purposes and who added to my knowledge of wild flowers in areas far beyond the Don Valley.

It is to be hoped that somehow we still restore a few slopes where all of our once plentiful wild flowers may be seen and appreciated. A woodland without wild flowers is as empty and desolate in some respects as a community without children. The flowers were here before us milleniums ago and they will remain with us if we just give nature a chance. If we do that small thing, she will do the rest.

CHAPTER TWENTY-ONE

Don Valley Birdmen

The soft "coo-coo-coo" of a mourning dove can be heard coming from a tree a short distance from where these notes were written. It reminds me that the mourning dove is a comparative newcomer to the Don Valley. The cardinal was unknown, at least to me, in the Valley during the '30s and it was only in the '50s that I heard and saw my first pileated woodpecker in the Don Valley.

Dozens of bird species drift past my windows during their spring and fall migrations. Other species take up housekeeping along the Valley slopes or in the spur ravines adjacent to them. While it is a great experience to be at Point Pelee during the bird migration in May, a similar phenomena may be observed within a few miles of downtown Toronto.

The birds are our friends. They need our protection and help. Thousands of people who appreciate nature now live along the crests of the Don Valley system, which has become a vast reservoir of bird life. We should keep it that way.

A simplified definition of an ornithologist is a person who is aware that watching bird species and bird life provides one of the most absorbing, restful and interesting occupations to which people can apply their leisure hours.

Naturalists who study birds and bird life see the Don Valley as a reservoir of bird species that might not otherwise be seen in East Toronto. This is true today despite the building of homes along the Valley and its spur ravines. The wooded slopes afford the nesting and feeding areas required by many species of birds. The Baltimore oriole, indigo bunting, red-eyed vireo, the flicker, veery kingfisher, and the catbird are among the species that can be seen within a mile or so of downtown Toronto. In the spring and fall the Valley becomes a route along which migrating birds travel to and from the south. One can see scarlet tanagers, cedar waxwings, white-throated sparrows and innumerable warblers. Even backyard gardens at some distance from the Valley are visited by these birds during migration.

Our winter birds enhance the drab weeks of the cold months. Blue jays, cardinals, juncos, chickadees, nuthatches and hairy and downy woodpeckers console us with their antics at the feeding boxes. Then with the return of spring, the robin is among the first of the birds to arrive from the south.

I was never much of a "birder" myself, although I loved birds and was on "speaking terms" with perhaps a hundred species. Two events were foremost among my cherished and anticipated signs of spring, namely seeing the bloodroot in flower and awaiting the arrival of the eastern bluebirds, who seemed to just drop from the sky to perch in a row on the wires of my fence line.

I actually had some success in raising bluebirds while at the Forks of the Don using a simple method. I nailed a large empty apple juice tin level with the top of the fence post. Then I nailed a piece of shingle or wood to the top of the post over the can to keep it watertight. Previously I had cut an entry hole about the size of a bluebird near the top of the can. I then nailed a forked twig to the post. It projected alongside of the entrance hole to serve as a perch. The bluebirds took to the tin cans and raised their broods in them. It was an idea I picked up somewhere in a magazine.

In early summer the bobolink invaded the fields of Donlands Farm. It was always a treat to see and hear bobolinks singing their heads off while swaying from sturdy weed stalks. These meadows are now all built up and you have to go further out into the country to see the bobolinks.

Kingfishers were common along the East Don River in the area of the Forks of the Don in the '20s and up until the '40s, then they disappeared. I was deeply gratified when in the late '70s I heard their familiar rattle along the Don near Beechwood Drive. I was skeptical at first but I indeed did see and hear them many times during my walks or while working the bee yard near the Don at Beechwood Drive. I don't know why the kingfishers came back but I suspect that small fish now present in the river may have had something to do with it. In all events, seeing the kingfishers was like the return of a long lost friend. I trust that some day the bluebirds will also return in number.

Stuart and Eleanor Thompson of Leaside were highly qualified ornithologists. Stuart was the author of several books about birds and one on rural fences entitled *Fences*. I have recollections as a young man, before I met Stuart, of listening to him imitate bird calls on a weekly radio program. He did this beautifully. Years later he imitated calls for me when I was fortunate enough to be hiking with him. Stuart was a salesman for Brigdens, a commerical art and printing materials firm. One day he was waiting in a large downtown office for the president of the company with whom he had an early afternoon appointment. There were probably 50 typists in the office, bent over their machines oblivious to anything but typing. Finally the president arrived. As he strode through the reception bay he said to Stuart, without so much as a glance at him, "Make a call like a loon." Stuart hesitated, whereupon the president turned to him and

Stuart L. Thompson.

repeated what he had said, "Go ahead. I mean it." Stuart obediently cupped his hands around his mouth and produced the weird, ghoulish laughing call of the loon with which tens of thousands of cottagers are familiar. The effect on the office was instantaneous. Everything stopped dead. It was an unexpected interruption in the business of the day that the typists probably never fogot. Stuart always chuckled when he told that story.

Stuart Thompson was, in my view, one of the best all-round naturalists Toronto ever produced. Stuart and his uncle, Ernest Thompson Seton, always rambled in the Don Valley on the latter's occasional visits to Toronto. Stuart personified the spirit of Don Valley rambles. He told me that he introduced the Honourable Dana Porter to the Don Valley, when the future cabinet minister was a small boy. "I took him by the hand," Stuart used to say.

Stuart was something of a loner. He would say, "You fellows make too much noise. You disturb the wildlife." So he rambled alone. One of Stuart's habits was swimming in the Don anytime of the year, even in January. Stuart simply plunged into the icy water, quite in the nude, splashed around, came out again and dried off with a handkerchief. He would then dress and saunter off as though nothing unusual had happened. He did this regularly. The Don, as all shallow steams, could be very cold in winter.

In the spring Stuart could be seen walking up the railway at dusk.

When I shouted over he would call back, "I am going to listen to the spring frogs." Soon after he would be seated by the edge of a pond, listening to the early spring sounds of the night. When the open countryside of Leaside, East and North York began to disappear under building lots, Stuart was saddened beyond words. He would confide to me, "Charlie, it's bad enough to look at, but to have to live with it is worse."

Stuart passed away first and Eleanor followed a few years later. One day their nephew Harold Thompson called me. "Charlie," he said, "I am disposing of things. You can have anything you want." It was as simple as that.

"Well," I said, "can I have Stuart's collection of slides?" This included hundreds of photos of birds, trees, flowers and butterflies, all mounted on glass. A tremendous collection, one that took a lifetime to put together. I promptly turned the slides over to the Metropolitan Toronto and Region Conservation Authority, who I knew would use them for educational purposes.

Thus passed from my life two very special people. Of Stuart it could be said that perhaps no one loved the Don better than he or had, in my time, known it longer, for Stuart was 20 years older than I. Some of the photos of the Don Valley, and one of my cottage in its original state, still in my collection, were taken by Stuart at a time when I had just recently entered this world.

Frank Smith was the first Don Valley bird carver I ever knew. He may have been the first in the Toronto region. Frank lived on one of the streets off Queen Street East near Pape. Like so many others he spent a lot of time in the Valley. A tall, strong, raw-boned man, Frank was also a deputy game warden. In this capacity he protected Valley trees and habitat. In those days there was a fellow or two who also trapped muskrat in the Valley under licence from the Department of Lands and Forests. Frank kept an eye on these trappers as well.

I never considered Frank a bird watcher, but he carved birds of every size and hue, beautiful enough to drive a bird lover frantic at the sight of them. In his workshop at home there were hundreds of these models, many of which were exhibited at the Canadian National Sportsmen's Show. Frank made a large contribution to the Don Valley Conservation Association. An article on Frank Smith appeared on the *Toronto Telegram*, July 17, 1945 and was entitled "Lifelike Birds Carved from Balsam".

Tom Russell was in my view "Mr. Birdman". He stuck to the Valley with the persistence of a shadow to a tree. Tom was a veteran of the First World War. He, like Ed Else, my brothers and many more veterans I had known, walked with an easy stride that identified a Canadian soldier at a glance. Time and again I saw Tom walking up the Valley, very much with the same steps that took him and his battalion along the roads during the last 100 days of 1918. Tom was a kind, uncomplicated man who enjoyed

Charles Sauriol, Stuart L. Thompson and Fletcher Sharp, February 1958.

the Valley's bird life with rewarding intensity. He knew where the long-eared owls were nesting in the ravine across from the cottage. He had discovered where the great horned owl was nesting. But the highlight of Tom's Don Valley bird experiences came during a late fall Sunday morning ramble. We both suddenly heard a loud screeching and saw to our amazement a pileated woodpecker fly over. That was the first time I had ever seen this bird in the Valley, although its chips and deep oblong holes, which could have been chiselled by a carpenter, had made us aware that the bird was somewhere in the vicinity.

With the formation of the Don Valley Conservation Association my favourite bird became the cardinal. We selected it as an emblem because it was colourful, a fighter and stayed with us during the winter. The cardinal was included in D.V.C.A. literature, was woven on the Association's badges and finally became the most visible bird insignia in the Don Valley. In the fifties I had two huge signboards cut in the outline of a male cardinal and painted accordingly. One of these signs was placed under the peak of my cottage at the Forks of the Don and was visible to traffic and to passengers riding the trains. The other sign was made for the de Grassi cottage and it too was highly visible. I still have those signs, although they are in different locations. The Don Valley Art Club included the signs in some of their murals, one of which may be seen in the East York council chambers.

Bob Speakman, the patrol officer for the Don Valley Conservation

Authority, was a regular visitor to my holdings. Bob assisted us in various ways. He made metal pheasant feeders which, when filled with grain, naturally attracted pheasants. In those days it was common to see flocks of 15 or more pheasants roaming the Valleys, even coming to the backyards of adjacent residences. These pheasants had been released as small birds and had thrived. Then they began to decrease in number and it is only occasionally that I now hear or see one. The brown ducks and mallards did better and may be seen now a hundred at a time in the river at the Forks of the Don.

The many accomplishments of the D.V.C.A. included the making of bird boxes. A local technical school entered into the spirit of things and Speakman masterminded the operation. The result was somewhat amusing for I inherited dozens of bird boxes of all kinds and shapes, all of which we eventually set up in appropriate locations. A chap by the name of Smith was responsible for setting up hundreds of bluebird boxes in the Metropolitan Toronto region and some of these were located along the headwaters of the Don.

INTRODUCTION TO PART THREE

The four following stories are my bee stories, three of which were selected from articles written by me for bee journals.

The first of these articles is about a few roots of thyme that Eleanor Thompson of Leaside gave me and which had since spread far and wide. This is followed by an account of a rescue mission to save John McArthur's beehives from destruction. The third story tells how John Jones' apiary was dismantled because of complaints from a scantily-clad maiden who wanted to make a vegetable garden alongside John's beehives. Finally there is a new story about my efforts to start a bee garden in the Don Valley. This led indirectly to the discovery that my bees had been gathering nectar from the white flowers of the poison ivy. These flowers did indeed produce some of the finest honey I had ever tasted.

So as stories go, the readers of *Tales of the Don* may well savour through my tales of bees some of the romance and breathe some of the folksy atmosphere that inevitably arises from the work of a hobbyist beekeeper in the sequestered valley of the Don.

While writing these lines I saw 20 acres of mustard in full flower near Coldwater, Ontario. What an adventure, I thought, to have a hive or two in that field. Could there be mustard honey? Yes, indeed. The bee flower manual informs me that mustard (*Brassica nigra*) produces a light amber honey with a yellow cast, mild in flavour but thin. I hope some day to spread mustard honey on my toast.

CHAPTER TWENTY-TWO

Mrs. Thompson's Thyme Lives On

I first became interested in Thymus vulgaris, *otherwise known as thyme, through Eleanor Thompson, wife of Stuart L. Thompson. The Thompsons lived in Leaside across the Valley from me. After Stuart's death I organized outings in which Eleanor participated. One day when I called for her she was thinning one of the flower borders and had gathered several handfuls of thyme roots which had overrun their alloted space. "Don't throw them away," I said. "Let me have them to plant at my cottage." That was the beginning of my kingdom in thyme.*

Within a summer or two the roots Eleanor had given me had grown into mats of verdure that grew in ever-widening circles. I began to subdivide these mats and the new plantings grew well. In no time it seemed I had a long border of thyme at the de Grassi place and had begun to set out other borders as well. I was quick to perceive that my bees were attracted to the flowers, which appeared early in July and remained for about a month. There were two species, one flowering ten days after the first. For several years I planted and transplanted thyme, setting out roots in every conceivable corner.

When the de Grassi property in the Don Valley was expropriated in 1968, I relocated four miles north of Tweed. My herbs went with me, including several bushel baskets full of thyme roots. My new dwelling stood on a gentle slope, which I felt would be a good place to plant thyme. By the summer of 1979 this slope, which measured about 60 feet long by 20 deep, was fully carpeted with thyme. The slope supplied me with all the stock I needed to start other borders and to plant thyme around the flat rocks on my property. In July thyme becomes a solid carpet of lavender, pink, deep purple and white flowers which the bees assail by the hundreds. The buckwheat odour of thyme flowers greets me each time I step out of the house on a warm, sunny July day.

Nature was quick to lend a hand in support of my efforts to propagate thyme. In my walks I would come unexpectedly upon a little self-sown patch of thyme pushing its way wherever fancy took it. Soon the thyme began to creep into the cottage lawn. A retired English army officer asked me, "Have you ever grown a lawn of thyme? If you do, it will be like walking on a carpet." And it was. The thyme began to grow here and there in the lawn and gradually spread, the seeds having been carried there by birds or by the wind. In some areas thyme had already replaced the grass and I have encouraged it to do so.

At nursery prices I could have become wealthy if I had sold some of the roots. However, through my articles in bee journals and by word of mouth, more people learned of the benefits of this useful garden herb. I began to give thyme away by the basketful to Canadian beekeepers and cottagers, along with a few suggestions as to what to do with it. Inquiries came in from the United States, to which I responded by sending them thyme seed. It was easy to gather. The dried stalks were cut with garden shears and then spread on newspaper in my greenhouse, whereupon the seed was shaken from them by the handful.

I have no record of how widespread my thyme has become. In 1981, having again resumed beekeeping in the Don Valley, I began to make a bee garden consisting of borders of nectar-bearing plants. Several of these borders were planted in thyme. Again the process of many years before was repeated and again my bees assailed the flowers for their nectar. As thyme is a valuable and attractive herb, I began planting it in the Valley. I tied small bunches of thyme root with string, a hundred or so of these bunches at a time, and planted them at intervals along my favourite trails where they will add a measure of floral beauty.

My interest in thyme reminds me that 50 years ago sweet rocket was sold in the seed stores as a garden flower, along with petunia seed and the other flower varieties gardeners habitually bought. About 25 years ago, sweet rocket "jumped the fence" and began to invade the river valleys and particularly river flood plains. In June acres and acres of fragrant lavender, pink or white sweet rocket flowers may be seen along the Don Valley Flood plains. In certain areas daffodils and English primroses are also running wild. One of my experiments includes a wildflower mixture which contains a species of calendula, which flowers from July to November and could possibly thrive as a wild plant.

Now, on a hot July afternoon, my nostrils are greeted with the scent of buckwheat, my eyes refreshed with the deep purple and light reds of the thyme flowers and my ears filled with the soothing droning of the bees. At such times it is pleasant indeed to bend over the patches of flowering thyme and watch the bees rifle the flowers of their nectar, nectar which will in some measure flavour their honey. Mrs. Thompson's thyme does indeed live on.

CHAPTER TWENTY-THREE

The Rescue of John McArthur's Bees

On Friday afternoon, May 1, 1958, the Ontario Honey Producers Co-operative, located on Defries Street in Toronto, were informed by the construction superintendent working on the Bayview extension that beehives were directly in the way of the construction crews. The owner had walked off the property. If the bees weren't moved by Tuesday, the superintendent informed them, he would set fire to the hives.

The Co-op called me. As I was familiar with the area, could I render the Co-op a service and check the situation? I called Stan Fisher, a Don Valley neighbour who kept bees, and we went to the apiary to investigate. Thirty-two beehives stood at the entrance to the Rosedale ravine, nailed together with long boards. The beehives were still in their winter packing of leaves, sacking and tar paper. This material should have been removed a month before. The bee yard had a dilapidated, desolate look about it. Equipment, which included a honey extractor, bee boxes (supers) and bee frames, was scattered over the ground.

Before meeting with Fisher, I called the *Globe and Mail* and asked if they were interested in a story about 600,000 bees blocking the extension. They were and assigned a press photographer and a writer to cover the story. Fisher and I began removing several hives and were in the act of putting one of them in a wheelbarrow when the *Globe and Mail* photographer and reporter arrived. They took a picture of the two of us and this picture appeared in the paper on Monday morning. There was the photo of Fisher and me with the hives and above the picture the newspaper headline, "750,000 Workers Bar Way to Bayview Extension". The article was a sensation. That evening Fisher and I salvaged two hives each and took them to our respective apiaries.

The next day, May 2, I returned to the bee yard with Syd Pugh of Pickering, C.R. Purcell of Rouge Valley and Bob Speakman. On that occasion I salvaged another colony, Pugh and Purcell each took three. It was quite a sight to see C.R.'s vehicle laden with beehives and equipment moving slowly over the Don Flats in the moonlight.

News of this kind spreads quickly. By Tuesday all 32 hives had disappeared. The salvage operation had been a success and the hives saved. I felt elated, for it would have been a pity to have destroyed them.

However, on Wednesday, the Co-op called me and said they hoped they had not caused me any trouble. "Why?" I asked. Apparently the Metro property department had called and claimed the bees as their own. Later, about mid-June, John McArthur called me. He was the nephew of the John McArthur I had known. He had seen the newspaper article and read about my part in the rescue. He was in dispute with Metro over a property settlement and the bees were part of the property in question. The land and the bees had been expropriated and he wanted a fair price. I told him what had happened and said that I would return the bees I could account for. But he didn't want that. By this time I was beginning to have misgivings about the role I had played in the whole affair.

A year passed and the incident seemed to have been quite forgotten. Then in early May two gentlemen from the Metro Toronto property department called at my office. There was to be a court hearing to establish the value of the apiary. They felt that the price claimed was a little high. They could establish this point by having a witness, namely myself, who was familiar with the apiary at the time of expropriation, testify at the hearing. "Oh no," I said, "not me." "See you in court," they responded. There I was, neatly trussed up in a bag, with the prospect of taking sides against the nephew of a man for whom I had great respect. However, if I was going to court I was going to tell the truth.

The court case proved to be an interesting event. I stayed with the facts, first relating what the McArthurs had done for Don Valley beekeeping. I admitted to having acted hastily, as I well knew that bees could not be moved from one location to another without a permit from the Department of Agriculture at Guelph University. But there had been an element of urgency which I couldn't ignore. The bees were to be destroyed by Tuesday and I wanted to prevent this. Furthermore the apiary was in sad condition and had to be attended to. The testimony was all that could have been asked for and I tried to be fair to McArthur. The final property settlement was fair. I called McArthur but he didn't want the bees. He had only wanted a fair settlement and there the matter ended.

In the aftermath of the hearing we had many a laugh about getting those hives out of the way of the extension and being stung in the process, for the operation was done mostly by flashlight or moonlight. But the scene that still stands out is that of C.R. Purcell's vehicles laden with beehives and equipment, silhouetted in the moonlight as it moved slowly across the Don Flats to Pottery Road.

Today, many years later, traffic moves along the Bayview extension in an unending stream. There remains not a trace of McArthur's presence and none of the vanished 750,000 worker bees which on that far-off day of May 1, 1958 posed a threat to the superintendent of the crews working on the extension who threatened to destroy them.

McArthur's bees deserved a better fate than they seemed headed for, a sentiment which cost me a few evenings not a few stings and a day in court with a *per diem* of $15, which I never collected.

CHAPTER TWENTY-FOUR

The Demise of John Jones' Bees

I lived in the Don Valley above Pottery Road. All of the residences on the west side were situated on ravine lots sloping into the Valley. A neighbour, John Jones, kept bees at the base of his lot for about 20 years. The slope on his property was steep and had a difficult access. To reach his bees more easily, John built a lift with a reversible motor. Roller skates turning on two smooth boards, one on each side of a stairway, provided the necessary momentum. A double length of cord wound or unwound on a roller to ensure that the lift could be lowered or raised only the length of the stairway.

The bee yard was almost inaccessible to anyone but John, who controlled the lift. Even so, the location was too close to neighbouring dwellings. Occasionally a rampaging bee stung someone, but there were no complaints and John's bees were free to bring to their hives the nectar of the lower Don Valley.

For quite some time my only contact with John had been to exchange bee talk with him. However, when I moved my bees from the Don Valley to Tweed, I began to give him a hand with his bee yard. This consisted of keeping the colonies in order and in assisting with the removal and extracting of the honey. We worked well together. All I wanted for my effort was to keep my hand in bees and to give a much older man the assistance he needed. This arrangement continued for several years. John was as proud of his apiary as could be. He sold the honey to Todmorden Mills pioneer village, where it found a ready market among his friends.

The bee season of 1978 started very much as other seasons, with ten strong colonies of bees. With July heat in May, they soon began to fill the hives with honey. By mid-June we had taken off 400 pounds of honey and it seemed like only the beginning. John, as though sensing some impending unfavourable situation, urged me to take some of the colonies for a new apiary I had started near Stouffville. He no longer felt up to keeping ten hives and felt that he was imposing on me, to whom had fallen the management of these hives.

Up until then John had never experienced any serious trouble with his neighbours, for although the lots all ran to the Valley, the bottom parts of most of the lots were not in use. However, a young lady living nearby fancied that she would like to have a vegetable garden. In addition to the benefits of working the soil, the young lady felt that she should also experience the benefits of the warm sunshine on her scantily clothed body. So in due course rows of radishes and spinach began to appear a few yeards from the ten beehives. Successful beekeeping presupposes the art of knowing when not to work the bees. But no matter how the beekeeper tries, there are times when bees will become upset and the guard bees will go looking for someone on whom to wreak their vengeance. This is why an apiary should be placed safely away from human habitation. Late in June the irate guards soon found their prey. What more convenient target than a bare-backed young lady bending over a hoe in the full glare of the sun. A few stings capped matters and the repercussions were catastrophic for John's bees.

We were approaching the First of July holiday weekend and the bees were at full strength, bringing in honey literally by the pailfull. Also the colonies were strong with brood. Of all times this was the wrong time to move bees. Unfortunately John was not in a strong legal position. There seemed nothing else to do but move the hives.

Moving those hives was my worst experience in beekeeping and was a crime against nature. Rape would be a more descriptive word for what we did. The hives were taken apart, packed in special boxes and carried away. We lost and destroyed hundreds of bees, broke up the brood pattern and totally disorganized the colonies at their high-tide of productivity. So many bees were left behind that John had to turn the hose on them to destroy them before they started rampaging up and down the street. The man of the hour was my veteran beekeeper friend, Hugh McLeod, who provided the special equipment and truck that made it possible to move the colonies. Some of these colonies were conveyed to Stouffville and others to Manvers. I estimated that the hives were worth at least $300 each before they were moved and it would have taken years to rebuild the apiary as it was.

I still have recollections of clusters of milling, edgy, irate, disorganized, angry, sting-minded bees who, despite our efforts to "smoke them quiet", stung us through our garments. It took us the entire First of July weekend to complete the moving. I had more bee stings than a man is entitled to have on the weekend of Canada's national holiday. It was all very sad and John took it to heart, for the bees had been his way of life. "Look, Charlie," he said, and pointed to the 14 supers (boxes), each containing 50 pounds of honey that we had removed as part of the spring crop. It was all rather pathetic, this break up of an old man's world, and John never quite got over it. He often thought of the heaps of drowned bees when during the winter he looked sadly out of his kitchen window to the unused lift. He knew that come spring there would be no bees to attend to at the bottom of the steps.

Toward the end of the moving operation I made my way down the steps to recover a bee brush I had left behind. While searching for it in

153

the thickening darkness I suddenly became intensely aware of the silence that had fallen over the place. Gone was the humming sound of congregated bees, gone the hive smell of newly processed honey that I love so much. Only the chirping of the early crickets could be heard.

At that moment I yearned for the folksy atmosphere of John's apiary, for the pungent odour of sumac smoke pouring from the smoker, for the sight of hundreds of bees darting to and from the hives, for the nostalgia of bee work from spring to fall and finally for those homespun bits of conversation between two beekeepers exchanging notes.

The vegetable garden did not last long. When the bees had been removed the groundhogs took over and I am sure that what was left was not worth twenty-five cents. The young lady simply gave up her garden.

As for John, he was terminally ill. He often thought of his First World War experiences with Welsh regiment. "I was the youngest fellow to enlist in the regiment. I lied about my age," he told me. But for all of his war experiences and despite the many houses he had built, for John was a master carpenter, beekeeping had meant the most to him. John had had a good thing going for himself but alas, no one living in a built-up area can create a nuisance and remain within the law. All beekeepers are amply protected by the Bees Act but John's beehives were just too close to his neighbours, one of whom was allergic to bee stings. To move the hives was a wise decision indeed. Furthermore the hives' survival was only a matter of time for John was already in his decline when the incident related in this chapter occurred. Most of his usefulness as a beekeeper came from his memories of better days.

John was never the same after he lost his bees and within two years he passed away. His widow called me one day and said, "Charlie, please take everything you can use. Please! Of all people, you are the one John would want to have the equipment." By that time I was back in bees so I gratefully carried away everything that could be used. That was the end of John Jones' apiary and the beginning of a new one, through which John Jones' memory lingers on and on.

CHAPTER TWENTY-FIVE

Poison Ivy Honey

Two species of the snowberry shrub may be found growing in the Don Valley: the small or wild species at the Forks of the Don where nature placed it long ago, and the larger or domestic kind which grows extensively at Todmorden Mills on the site of the de Grassi homestead and more recently, that is a few years ago, on wild land near Beechwood Drive. All of these domestic plantings were started by me.

In 1957 I was instrumental in securing for the Metropolitan Toronto Conservation Authority a parcel of 78 acres of picturesque land near Glen Major. A large patch of the domestic snowberry stood near a pioneer dwelling on the property. The snowberry produces hundreds of new shoots with roots which are easily transplanted. In the course of events I lifted quite a number of these shoots and, knowing how attractive the small pink snowberry flowers were to bees, hoped to get the shrub started in the Don Valley, which I did.

It was probably from this modest beginning that I began to plan a bee garden. How practical indeed to bring together in one location all of the plants with nectar-bearing flowers and arrange them in borders and in massive plantings. The bees would have easy access to these flowers which, being near the hives, would save the bees time in the usual search for nectar. A steady flow of nectar in the hives from many kinds of flowers could result in new blends of honey.

It took many years for the concept of a bee garden to evolve, for my experiments were first on a small scale with just a few plants. Then as my awareness of plants increased, I also began to grow them from seed. Matters were at this stage when in the spring and summer of 1981 I was able to establish my garden on a larger scale quite close to home. This was done on a two-acre parcel of wild land enclosed by a link-chain fence. Part of this story is related in an earlier chapter in this book. The response to what seemed so simple a plan came as a surprise. *A Beeman's Journey* was introduced and written up with much fanfare and was talked about over the radio. Apparently many people thought that centralizing honey plants for the convenience of the bees was quite a good idea and felt that it should be practised on a wide scale. It was something that could be done by hobbyist beekeepers with just a few hives located in areas where there was little bee pasture for the bees to visit. Such situations could be corrected by bringing in plants and by sowing honey plant seed, especially clover, extensively.

I merely wanted to make the Valley more attractive than before. Instead of certain species of coarse weeds, which produce nothing, there could be fields ablaze with colour and with the added value of providing a source of nectar for the bees.

But there remain many things to learn from my experiment. This could well be the first time in the history of the Don Valley that bees emerging from their hives are confronted with masses of tempting nectar-laden plants which they can visit easily. However the bees may just as easily prefer to do things the hard way, ignore my borders of bounty and fly a mile or more in pursuit of some other kind of fowering plant that takes their fancy. Only time will tell.

Nevertheless my past experiments with mass plantings of thyme, motherwort, catnip and other nectar-laden flowers within yards of my hives have proven successful and the flowers have been literally crawling with bees. Yet the question remains: if a bee has a choice of basswood flowers growing over yonder, why do they at times pass them by for the milkweed flowers just down the road? The answer will come as we keep on learning and passing on our experiences to others.

In the summer of 1982 no plant was further from my thoughts in terms of honey than the despised and feared poison ivy. This plant, as most of us know, produces glossy leaves in the summer and clusters of white berries in the fall.

The berries are produced from small white flowers which, unknown to me, were nectar-bearing. I had not observed that these flowers were visited by bees. The discovery that bees gathered poison ivy nectar provided me with one of the strangest experiences in my career as a beekeeper. Part of the story is related in *A Beeman's Journey* but a few references to the experience are made here.

The excellence in flavour and colour of a batch of late summer honey which I was unable to identify prompted me to have it analyzed by the University of Guelph. I was informed several months later that my product was poison ivy honey and could be consumed safely.

I concluded that the bees had been gathering poison ivy nectar since they were first brought into the Don Valley but it was lost in the general flow of nectar into the hives. Some unusual situation was undoubtedly present in the summer of 1982 that caused the bees to concentrate on the flowers of the poison ivy. Perhaps some plants did not yield nectar that year. The cycle which caused this situation may not recur in a long, long while and I may never extract a batch of poison ivy honey again. In this event a few jars from my stock have been set aside to provide me with evidence to support one of the strangest occurrences in my career as a beekeeper.

What may seem strange to us is not strange to nature. The bees instinctively know what flowers to visit. If the leaves of the poison ivy cause skin eruptions and produce painful itching, the flowers in nature's plan produce nectar for one of the finest honeys one could wish to taste.

Lest Old Acquaintance be Forgot

This section includes observations about three men who, each in his own time, often walked Don Valley trails with me. They were Eric La Trobe, J.D. Thomas and Dr. Fletcher Sharp. These three were particularly close friends and each in his own way made major contributions to my career and success as a conservationist. Each shared my love for the Don Valley and the abundance in nature it embodied.

There comes to mind some lines written by me following the loss a short while ago of a esteemed associate of the Nature Conservancy of Canada, the late Anna Louis Martin:

> *"The making of a friend presupposes the possibility of losing that friend, for which we must be prepared. Mortal loss is life's most frustrating blow: for years we share our talents then it is over, gone forever, beyond recall. Yet the phantom of the friendship is still there like the void of an amputated limb, a will of the wisp haunting the memory of days gone by, never to return. From this comes one simple truth: to cherish what we have while we have it, for the paths that are now shared by two may one day be traversed alone."*

CHAPTER TWENTY-SIX

Eric La Trobe

I wrote the following lines on January 3, 1957 in my column, "Diary of a Conservationist":

> *"Today a truck was driven up my driveway loaded with beekeeping equipment. It was a gift from a friend who shortly after the war took a lease on a run-down dwelling, decrepit barn and a few weed infested acres north of Uxbridge, which he called "Starve Crow Farm". The boards of the dwelling had so warped that air passed between them like water through a sieve.*
>
> *"My friend kept chickens which never seemed to lay eggs, geese which merely shrieked or waddled to the pond, a goat which produced no milk, and had a garden plot whose soil had petered out. Fortunately fishing in the brook that flowed through the property was good and the wild raspberries nearby grew in abundance, which we ate swimming in country cream from a neighbouring farm.*
>
> *"One winter at Starve Crow was enough for my friend. Come spring he and his wife moved to the second floor of a general store at the four corners of nowhere, bringing with them several 40-pound pails of honey, payment for assistance rendered to a local beekeeper. Somehow one of these pails tipped over during the night and the honey leaked through the floorboards into the general store below, much to the consternation of the storekeeper."*

My friend was the uncle Eric whose stories, concocted by me, appeared in *The Cardinal* back in the early fifties and more recently in *Remembering the Don*. Uncle Eric was Eric La Trobe, my hiking companion during the 1930s and into the mid-forties.

I met Eric La Trobe in the Don Valley quite by accident. I was out on a ramble with my dog Mousse over a trail through a hemlock grove. Suddenly the dog disappeared over a rise in a trail and began barking. I caught up with the dog, who was barking at a middle-aged man and four teenaged youths. We struck up a conversation. I learned that La Trobe was a scoutmaster and these were boys from a Rover crew enjoying the civic holiday weekend camping up the Don. I invited him to pay us a visit at the cottage, which he did that evening. La Trobe was the prototype of the kindly scoutmaster, well versed in the outdoors and with a deep interest in the young lads who engaged in Rover crew activities. We became firm friends from the start and for many years he was my constant hiking companion, dependable and, as woodsmen go, one of the best.

At the time I was engaged in compiling a history of the Don, a laborious, time-consuming project that took some 20 years. To compile the text for this history it was necessary to walk along the two Valleys of the Don from end to end. This effort was more rewarding when La Trobe, and sometimes Herb Staples, son of Owen Staples, the artist, accompanied me. We progressively explored the river valleys to their headwaters, the upper reaches of which were often new to me.

While in the process of exploring the Valleys for my history, we identified places where we could make camp and have lunch en route. These places became focal points for individual rambles. They bore fanciful names, including "Upturned Root", which was a shelter under a massive upturned root, "Cup-in-the-Hill", "Hemlock Point", and "Juniper Hill". We felt at times like traders checking our line of outposts.

In time we added night hikes to those of the weekends. While this may seem at this late date like kids' stuff, it actually wasn't. I felt it would be beneficial to get away from the city and business duties for one evening a week, usually Wednesday, trek up the Don to a sheltered place, throw up a fire and relax for several hours, which is exactly what we did.

La Trobe was absolutely dependable and as good natured as could be. He could climb a tall pine tree like a sailor going up a mast and often did so to break off pieces of dead branches, which he threw to the ground while I made the fire. Even today, some 50 years later, I become nostalgic with the memory of those irreplaceable evenings. Imagine a comfortable seat of boughs with a clear view across the Valley to the east, with scarcely a glimmer of a light. The therapeutic value of leaving one's concerns for a few hours, of sitting before a cheerful blaze with the hushed quiet of the night, the crackle of the fire, the resinous scent of the pine knots burning, the call of a saw-whet owl and the incandescent light of the moon for company was tremendous. It restored my sense of well-being more than anything else I could have done. Men by the dozens will tell you of experiencing comparable emotions in Algonquin Park but we enjoyed these experiences in the Don Valley, a scant half-hour from home.

The moon was a beautiful sight by these nightfall firesides. Often we saw the orb rise majestically over the tips of the white pine trees, silhouetted against the rim of the Valley to the east. It is difficult to convey the sheer beauty of moonlight cast against a natural scene to someone who has not experienced its charm. The anticipation of a moonlit walk or of sitting by a fire in full moonlight was such that for many years I planned

Evening fireside up the Don, circa 1936.

my business trips to ensure that I would be in Toronto each month during the period of the first quarter to full moon. La Trobe made these outings possible for there were few people I knew who enjoyed this sort of thing. It should be said, however, that today cross country skiers seem to relish the prospect of a moonlight run on skis. Such an event can bring out 30 or more people at a time.

Eric La Trobe played an important role in my life. He was a skier of a sort, having learned to use skis while in the army. As he put it, he was a walker on skis but sufficiently skilled to ski to whatever areas we wanted to reach. He also had some training in beekeeping. It was through La Trobe that I met J. Rice Murphy, or "Old Murph", the Don Valley beekeeper. When La Trobe first met him he kept bees near what is now Bayview Avenue near Eglinton. Through Murphy I met William (Bill) Dennison, one-time mayor of Toronto, who was also a beekeeper.

La Trobe's personal life is not for this story, other than to mention that after a period of trying to find his niche in the community, and marrying the woman who could help do the most for him, he settled down to a comfortable lifestyle. He remained our family's cherished friend until his death.

There were two children from La Trobe's marriage and the boy, Jamie, became the little Jamie of "Uncle Eric's Christmas Tree". It was written originally for *The Cardinal*, Winter 1951, and reproduced in *Remembering the Don*, p. 28-30. The first lines read:

The house at Starve Crow farm, Leaksdale. La Trobe and friends on doorstep.

*"His heart was full of love and goodwill
for the little creatures of Juniper Hill . . . ."*

Actually Eric and I did set up a Chritmas tree for the birds, as I required this authenticity of experience to put proper feeling in the words to be composed. On the Saturday before Christmas La Trobe and I set out for Juniper Hill with a bag full of pieces of bread, suet, bacon ends and other tidbits. Juniper Hill lay on the edge of the Valley, directly above the river on the western end of Lawrence Avenue East Don Valley Bridge. On arriving on the site we selected a medium sized spruce tree and began hanging the morsels on branches. A few days later everything had completely disappeared, as was to be expected. We derived much pre-Christmas pleasure from this. The birds had a special festive lunch and a magazine feature article about the exploit was written by me.

My diary of the thirties is full of the doing of Eric La Trobe, for I carefully recorded our outings and conversations. I am hopeful that these notes may some day be brought to light, as they are deeply undercut with humour. For example, on a Sunday in July La Trobe left my residence in shorts, carrying a set of skis on his shoulder. He walked all the way to Union Station to have the skis shipped east, completely indifferent to the sensation he was creating.

Our pre-Christmas rambles were always enlivened by my efforts to gather material for personalized Christmas cards. I sometimes went to unusual lengths, as the cards were based on outdoor scenes. Once I tied a bit of cedar foliage to a card with red ribbon, along with a small candle. The message was written on birch bark which was pasted to paper stock that resembled wood. I have a photo of one card which has pasted to it a photo of a section of white birch tree, with my hand etching and my name in charcoal on the birch bark. This sort of craftsmanship brought great pleasure but required patience when the cards were produced in quantity. However, it was a pastime which sat well with celebrating the season as best as we might.

Understandably it was a shock to me when Eric La Trobe passed away. But memory of him has never faded, nor will it ever. He was an unpretentious man and by my standards a great Canadian who, like so many hundreds of kindred souls, joined the ranks of the lovers of the Don Valley. Today he rests in the little churchyard at Whitby, in view of Highway 401, not too far from the harbour where his Rover crew once plied the oars of a lifeboat that La Trobe had somehow put his hands on to help shape the future of those fine young men.

CHAPTER TWENTY-SEVEN

J.D. Thomas

On the Sunday afternoon before Christmas 1950 I responded to a knock on my front door to be greeted by J.D. Thomas and his son Doug. "Charles," J.D. said, "I want to set your mind on fire." (This was a familiar approach.) "The Don Valley Conservation Association needs a mouthpiece, a publication to carry its news and to tell and sell its story of conservation. With your background in the publishing business and your skills as a writer, you are the man to put it together." So saying, he walked away.

My first contact with J.D. had been through a letter from the Ontario Conservation Association, of which he was honorary president. As a resident of Don Valley Drive, he had heard about the activities of the newly formed Don Valley Conservation Association. He made it clear that if there was anything he could do, he would. During my early meetings with him I learned that he had served as an artillery officer in the First World War and that he had filled the post of federal Deputy Minister of Labour during the Second World War. On April 25, 1941 he served as chairman of the Guelph Conference.

It is well known that great tracts of southern Ontario had been ruined through over cutting of the forest and through faulty farming practices. Representative conservation groups were called together to find a solution. J.D. felt that a conservation program should be launched to serve the dual purpose of providing employment and of restoring the damaged environment.

As a result of the Guelph Conference the Ganaraska rivershed was selected for a pilot study, with the objective of restoring the natural values of the watershed, which was one of the most damaged in the province. The restoration of the Ganaraska watershed was the beginning of the conservation authorities of Ontario. The Conservation Authorities Act was passed in 1946. It seems more than coincidental that a man of J.D.'s calibre, who had served as midwife for the conservation authorities movement, should come into my life at a time when we were struggling to launch the Don Valley Conservation Association. I could not have wished for a better pillar on which to lean. J.D. was a fighter, a man who had been through the mill, who had an utter disdain for people who speculated in real estate. He saw in me someone who could pick up where he had left off. He told me once, "I am on the way out, you are on the way in. Make the most of it."

On that December day in 1950 J.D. had set another of his carefully laid traps for me. He knew that if I took up the challenge of the publication he had in mind, I would see it through. The concept of a publication was excellent. We had launched a few issues of *Valley Don*, propelled by the enthusiasm of Roy Cadwell, but publication petered out. By the following week I had prepared a format of a sort for the new magazine and went to work on it. I had in mind an eight-page periodical. It was to be known as *The Cardinal*. Terry Short of the Royal Ontario Museum designed the motif for the front page. There were to be four issues, in spring, summer, fall and winter. The publication would carry association news and there would be conservation stories and articles on Don Valley history as well. The first issue, which appeared in the spring of 1951, was an acceptable effort. The second issue established the format that would remain during *The Cardinal*'s lifetime. J.D.'s comment was, "You have proven what you can do." – and that summarizes his contribution to the magazine.

Up until 1950 my energies had been centered on the Don Valley. J.D.'s concerns ranged further afield and he prepared me for the greater challenges that lay ahead. By the early summer of 1951 the rehabilitation of the Ganaraska watershed was well underway. On July 19, 1951 J.D. took me to see his handiwork. We met Ed Youngman, the Durham forest manager, in Orono and proceeded with the site visit. Here is what I wrote at the time, as it appeared in *The Cardinal*, Fall 1951:

"We 'Jeeped' along forest glens, up eroded gullies, and up to the dominating point of Tower Hill some 2,000 feet above sea level commanding a magnificent view of the area immediately north of Lake Ontario near Port Hope. During the four hours of brushing aside branches and pushing sand, we saw some outstanding achievements in conservation. It did one's heart good to see the bare sand hummocks of other years, the one-time gullies of clay, now planted in pine and black locust. Two million trees have been planted on the Ganaraska since 1947. A brief comment about our friend of conservation. J.D. Thomas was one of the guiding lights which led the Ganaraska project to a successful conclusion. On the site visit Ed Youngman took us to an historic spot, the place where the first reforestation tree was planted in the Ganaraska. Ed produced a copy of the Toronto Telegram *of May 15, 1947 and read these lines from the paper:*

'Twenty Thousand Acre Forest for Ganaraska Watershed
Ceremony near Port Hope launches a great project to

*reclaim vast sand areas. After a speech by the Honoura-
ble Dana Porter [then Minister of Planning and Develop-
ment], J.D. Thomas, Honorary President of Ontario
Conservation Association said, "By planting trees at the
source of the river, the stream will be slowed right down
to a walk in the spring." Dedication of the forest was a
great day for Mr. Thomas, for it marked the realization
he had cherished since 1941 when he was chairman of the
Guelph Conference comprised of conservation experts
from all parts of the Province. Mr. Thomas, who was
instrumental in having the Ganaraska project completed,
said that he had been chided by his colleagues that not so
much as a blade of grass had been planted on the watershed. I'll plant a tree here myself, vowed Mr. Thomas, and
he did.'"*

At that time the slope on which Mr. Thomas stood was bare of trees.
When we saw it during our visit it was covered with a young thriving forest of fast-growing Carlina poplar trees. Today the Ganaraska watershed
is one of the largest forested areas of southern Ontario.

It was on the Ganaraska and subsequent site tours that J.D. shared
his vision of what lay ahead. He did it in his own way, by shaping me
around the D.V.C.A., J.D. knew everyone who counted in conservation,
including A.H. Richardson, the chief conservation engineer. Between
them, with assistance from Roy Cadwell, a successful effort was made
to launch the Don Valley Conservation Authority. This was the official
body designated by the province and the municipalities to carry out a
master plan for the preservation of the Don River watershed. But alas,
an Authority is only as effective as the people who run it. The Don Valley Conservation report was made public on February 7, 1951. See *The
Cardinal*, Spring 1951, for particulars.

Meanwhile the D.V.C.A. continued in its role as the voice of the people. I recall vividly J.D. at our public functions, and particularly during
the train trips, in his Jack Canuck get-up, complete with Stetson hat,
frontiersman-type jacket, high boots, binoculars and cane. Behind this
pose could still be seen the typical army major whose mannerisms J.D.
was never able to shake. One July day, as we sat chatting on my terrace
overlooking the Valley, J.D. glanced across to the decaying white clay
walls of the "Ghost of Bayview", a caricature of Toronto that was known
from coast to coast. "Charles," he said, "what I would not give to have
my old battery here for five minutes and blow that g--d----d monstrosity
off the landscape."

By degrees we became firm friends. Marriages, it is said, are made
in heaven, friendships among conservationists are welded in footsteps
over the trails, through the wetlands and wherever there is a battle to be

J.D. Thomas at Vandorf Woodlot, 1953.

fought to save the landscape. J.D. was a shoulder-to-shoulder fighter, a fiery speechmaker who could hold his own in any municipal chamber or in the corridors of ministerial offices in Queen's park. When he set out with a definite idea of what he wanted, he got it. But the next day he became the quiet observant, deep-thinking man of the outdoors, with his favourite bird and wild flower books tucked in his hiking bag along with the binoculars. He attracted people and helped them on their way. John Bradshaw, known to so many Canadians, always greeted me before his talks in which I participated with, "Wouldn't J.D. be proud of this." He always said it with deep feeling, for John's career was launched by J.D. Similarly it was J.D.'s advice that guided Harry Boyle to his success as a writer and broadcast personality of note. J.D. told me that Rand Freeland, who was struggling with Fantasy Farm at the time, came to him one evening and said, "I'll sell the whole thing for $500." "I'll buy it," said J.D. The next day J.D. took the scribbled note of agreement back to Freeland and said, "Tear it up and get to work."

He told me of the effort he was taking to save the Guelph home of John McCrae, the poet who wrote "In Flanders Fields". I cannot recall the steps he took to do it. He is never mentioned in this connection but had he not intervened, John McCrae's home, in all likelihood, would not have been saved.

One lovely October we had just returned from a visit to the New England states and stopped for the night in an eastern Ontario motel. J.D.

always filled his thermos with coffee the night before. On this morning, sipping his coffee, he called over to me. "Charles, I would like to buy London Bridge." I said, "What?" All I could remember of London Bridge was the ditty we sang as children. I looked at him for a moment or two and he said, "No, I'm not crazy. It's for sale. The City of Toronto should buy it." In utter disbelief I learned that he had hit the nail on the head. London Bridge was for sale. It never fell down but was removed, a stone at a time, and shipped to Arizona where it stands today.

During our walks in the woods or visits to each others' homes, he would sometimes say, "You've got to raise a million dollars for conservation." In those days a million dollars was a lot of money and millionaires were relatively few. So, for a fellow like me, who counted his assets as a few thousand, raising a million dollars was like building an Egyptian pyramid. It was something I did not take seriously at the time but I used the idea in a novel I wrote (unpublished) entitled, "The Trail of the Golden Walnut". In this novel J.D. was the mayor of a small eastern Ontario city. He urges the hero (who is anybody's guess) to go out and raise a million. Well in the years that followed I played the major role in raising an estimated $6 million towards the purchase of natural area land and a much larger sum in gifts to the Crown.

J.D. was deadly serious about the preservation of natural values. "Wait," he would say, "until colour television comes on the market." We were not even talking about it at the time, but he foresaw it. Also he foresaw what the pictures of the natural landscape in colour could do to the cockles of people's hearts. Today not a week passes without nature programs appearing on the television screen in colour.

But his greatest achievement was undoubtedly the concept of the Golden Plow, linked with the International Plowing Match. It was based on the concept of beating swords into plowshares, often talked about but not too often put into practice. J.D. foresaw positive results from an international brotherhood of man based on food. There may have been other ways but J.D. gave it a try. His campaign took him to England and several other European countries. Holland was certainly one of them, for I recall the day he bought flowers in that country and had them sent over by plane to his family. "Imagine, Charles, being able to do that in a day. I bought them in the morning and they had them that evening." On several occasions I sprang to his defense, after he had passed away, when the Golden Plow was talked about with no mention of J.D. Thomas.

J.D. Thomas concealed a tenderness for natural beauty under a gruff exterior. He also had an obsession for early, meaningful retirement. The first was revealed to me during a fall visit to upper New York State. We were walking on the main street of a hamlet when he disappeared inside a church. A few moments later he beckoned to me and I entered the church. The rear wall of the church contained a very large picture window and within its view were the flamboyant colours of the autumn landscape reflected in the waters of a placid lake. "How would you like to preach a sermon to a congregation who could at will look past the preacher to a scene like that?"

J.D. was determined to retire at 60 years of age and did it skilfully. We had discussed early retirement as much as any subject. J.D. held the belief that many good men, forced into retirement too soon, should be re-established in business and go on to a second career. This notion resulted in another of J.D.'s brain children. Associated Senior Executives was launched in June 1958 by three retired executives. J.D. often said, "Too many men wreck themselves on retirement. They reach the promised land and all its goodness, still shackled or blessed with a lifetime of experience for which they have no further use. I am going to change that. Call it whatever you like, recycling of talent or rescuing a man from a slow walk to his doom, but I am going to change it." Preaching that doctrine took J.D. across the country as a guest speaker. Also it heaped blessings on many a couple, for 42 per cent of the calls for the company's services were from women who wanted to get their husbands out of the house. Retirement can only be enjoyed by a man or woman who has prepared a program well in advance.

By the early sixties, J.D. had begun to fail. I saw the physical change a long time before and from the realization that our time together was limited began the maturing of our friendship. By then I had made my mark with the Metropolitan Toronto and Region Conservation Authority and J.D. often accompanied me when I was looking over land on the Authority's behalf. He saw the results of Hurricane Hazel and the whirlwind for the preservation of the environment that it created.

Many a Saturday morning I called for him at his modest apartment on Bessborough Drive. I took him to Glen Major and to easily-reached points along the Don, and through the woods and wetlands north of Mount Albert, where one could ramble for a day. Late each afternoon I returned him to his apartment, tired and ever so pleased with the day. Then suddenly it was over; a brief hospitalization and that was the end.

I was asked if I would do the family a great honour and spread the ashes. It was Irma, his eldest daughter, who made the request. "No, Irma, really I couldn't. Not up the Don." She and Ralph understood. Fittingly they spread the ashes to the top of Tower Hill with a commanding view of the Ganaraska forest.

By 1980 I became concerned that J.D. would be forgotten unless steps were taken to keep his memory alive. I did this by assisting with the purchase of land along the Wilmot Creek to be dedicated to J.D. Thomas, A.H. Richardson and A.S.L. Barnes. A memorial service was held in June 1980 in the little church of Liskeard, adjacent to the property we had helped to buy. the plaque, unveiled that day and visible as one enters the church, bears this inscription:

TO THE NORTH LIES THE
WILMOT CREEK COMMEMORATIVE FOREST

acquired with the assistance of the Nature Conservancy of
Canada, the Ontario Conservation Authorities and the
Province of Ontario in honour of Dr. A.H. Richardson,
A.S.L. Barnes and J.D. Thomas, whose vision and
dedication contributed immeasurably to the conservation
movement in Ontario.

June 1980
GANARASKA REGION CONSERVATION AUTHORITY

CHAPTER TWENTY-EIGHT

Dr. Fletcher Sharp

I was working in my bee yard on the de Grassi lot in the spring of 1948 when Stuart Thompson passed by with a hiking companion whom he introduced as Fletcher Sharp, M.D. It was just one of those casual, quickly forgotten meetings that would have remained forgotten had I not decided to ramble along the crest of the Valley south of Eglinton Avenue. In so doing I unexpectedly encountered a group of four persons, Fletcher Sharp, Mrs. Sharp and Lew Owens and his wife. The group had been botanizing when a man came along with a big dog and ordered them off the property. It was the chap with the market garden across from my cottage. In an effort to redeem the good name of the Valley I agreed to share a ramble with Dr. Sharp at an early date.

There is no record of my first rambles with Dr. Sharp but in the ensuing two years we did ramble a great deal. On February 12, 1950 I noted that Stuart Thompson, Fletcher Sharp and I started down Valley from York Mills Road traversing unspoiled ravines to the Forks of the Don. We had lunch by a tiny brook in the woods of Milne's Hollow.

Then, on April 2, 1950, the three of us spent a day exploring the source of Boyle's Creek, which is the stream that flows through Richmond Hill and whose source I believed at the time lay in the McConnell cedar swamp by the Elgin Mills sideroad. By the end of 1950 we had established a pattern that was to hold in our excursions for a period of more than 30 years. It was a most extraordinary pattern of exploration of the outdoors, during which we systematically hiked over the woodlands of the metropolitan Toronto region and beyond. These rambles occurred weekly or semi-monthly, with intermittent breaks when the doctor left the city on holidays. Fletcher Sharp believed that a person should know his environment intimately within 20 miles of where he lived.

The doctor and I were two nature amateurs, interested in everything: geology, woodlands, birds, flowers. He would say, "Let's check this out." Or "Let's find out what it is." This practice made us familiar with all aspects of the outdoors.

In all likelihood we were among Ontario first cross country or trail skiers, although skiing as such was not widely known at the time. For a few years we had hiked until December, when the first heavy snowfall effectively sealed off the woods for comfortable walking. So one year I said, "Why dont' we get out our skis? They will get us easily through the woods." He agreed and henceforth we could go wherever we wished. In the mid-fifties ski equipment was cumbersome and crude. The skis were all made of wood and were wide and heavy. Likewise the boots, which could have served for hiking as well as skiing. But we got over the trails and particularly over the wetlands, which of course could not be walked over in summer, and visited the realm of muskrat, beaver and the ambling fox.

The renown of the Don Valley in the realm of skiing extended far beyond my wanderings on skis or the beginnings of the soon defunct East York Ski Club. The Toronto Ski Club, incorporated in 1924, used the Valley extensively, starting from the Rosedale Golf Club holdings. However the club needed a jump for the Ontario Championship Ski Meet held on February 12, 1934. A site was chosen on the west side of the Don Valley, directly across the Valley from the present Science Centre. The swath of cleared Valley slope is visible to this day on land included in the hydro right-of-way.

Two jumps were made, the main jump for competition and a smaller one for practice runs. I remember the meet quite well. I also recall meeting Charlie Durant, Alex Duncan and Sam Cliff, the guiding lights of the Club. The name of Sam Snively was later related to the acquisition of St. George's Lake through the M.T.R.C.A.

However in 1934 Thorncliffe seemed far enough from anywhere for the purposes of the meet. With the approach of the great event, nature performed perfectly as to temperature but failed to deliver the required snow. This detail was rectified by trucking in the white stuff in sufficient quantity to cover the ski slope.

The ski jump pictured in the *Star* of January 25, 1934 was a formidable affair and organizers said jumps of up to 150 feet could be made from it. Pictures of snow being trucked in and of the meet, which attracted 10,000 spectators, were featured in both the *Star* and the *Telegram* in their editions of February 12, 1934. Who today among the throngs which visit the Thorncliffe Plaza, or walk along the macadam footpaths that extend through the West Don Valley, have the faintest notion of the exciting spectacle that occurred there in 1934?

Summit, adjacent to the Gormley sideroad, could also, with some imagination, be included in the Don Valley system used by the Toronto Ski Club. This place, then remote, was festooned with trails built by the club and still in use today. Night skiing became a feature of Summit, with lights placed along some of the trails. The club, in its march to its 50th year and beyond, has gone farther afield but the local area, particularly the Don Valley, still remains very popular.

Seven years before the founding the Metropolitan Toronto Region Conservation Authority Fletcher Sharp and I were either walking or skiing over terrain that I was later destined to explore for conservation pur-

Dr. Fletcher Sharp with Charles Sauriol, December 1964.

poses. Occasionally we joined naturalist groups. On December 2, 1956 I noted that we had joined a group of hikers in a monthly nature ramble organized by the *Toronto Telegram*. Dr. Fletcher Sharp headed the botany group which tramped through the woods east of Aurora. Most often we rambled alone, with a style set to our rambling which included a pot of tea with lunch in a sheltered nook. The professional birders used to chide us when we met them. "Boy Scout stuff," they said. But they were more intense about birding than we were. However, we probably knew the regional woods as well as anyone. Freeing our minds of concerns was as stimulating as unlocking the secrets of the woods. In his declining years Fletcher would often say, "Do you think there are two fellows anywhere who have had as much fun exploring the outdoors as we have had?"

Never once in 30 years did I see him unruffled over any situation. Yet he could be elated beyond words by an unusual natural event. On a ramble along the Vandorf Creek we came across a saw-whet owl dozing on a cedar branch near the creek. Fletcher picked it up, stroked the bird tenderly and put it back on its perch. On an Easter Monday, while traversing open lands dotted with old pine stumps near Vandorf, about 30 grass snakes appeared from recesses under a stump, their tongues moving the while. This was the mother house in which the snakes had congregated for the winter. Soon they would disperse to their summer quarters but return to the stump in the fall. It seemed that we were able to record something of exceptional interest on every ramble.

Dr. Sharp followed my conservation work with interest and although the programs of the conservation authorities were not entirely clear to him, he predicted great changes in the landscape. He would say, "In a hundred years this will all be different. Every acre of land will be covered with trees and many of them will be species not growing here at present." I made it a point never to discuss business or personal problems on a ramble. These were to be nature rambles and this is perhaps why they are so well remembered.

For several years I wrote a weekly column, "Diary of a Conservationist", which included some of our explorations along the trails. The metropolitan Toronto region hinterland was a naturalist's paradise. Along with the river valley systems of the Credit, Humber, Don and Rouge, were the rolling hills of the interlobate moraine, the country of kettle lakes, of which there are perhaps a score. We saw this hinterland before development, although even today much of the area is still in a natural state. Even now, when on a tour, I tell my companions that many years ago Fletcher Sharp and I hiked through these woods. Naturally we met property owners, as we always sought permission to traverse their land. This generally resulted in a cup of coffee, a chat and considerable respect for Fletcher's position as a prominent downtown Toronto M.D.

What he did for me can only be inadequately expressed. He diagnosed people and I would venture to say that he could read me like a book. He would say, "You are so lucky. You inherited all of the best genes at the moment of conception." He believed that if you had health, you had everything.

One of our favourite walks and botanizing sites was what is now called the Wilket Creek ravine, connecting the west valley of the Don with Edwards Gardens. We reached the ravine from Don Mills Road about where the IBM offices now stand. From there we went across fields and through woods to the area presently traversed by the Leslie Street extension. The first factory to locate in the area was Barber Greene and the route and trail became known to Fletcher as the Barber Greene trail. The woods, which then covered the Leslie Street extension to the creek valley, were particularly attractive, wild and teeming with plant and bird life. In some respects it was like a jungle, particularly along the creek. Many times we followed its course until the tanglewood of natural scenery suddenly gave way to the beautifully landscaped Edwards' property, known for its graceful weeping willows and French water wheel, activated by the waters of the creek. The Edwards' dwelling, which has since been destroyed by fire, was on the crest of the ravine. In due course we became acquainted with Mr. Rupert Edwards and enjoyed coffee with him. Mr. Edwards, a distinguished gentleman connected with the Leaside Varnish Company, informed us with a smile that Mrs. Edwards felt that the property was too far from the city.

The following item appeared in my newspaper column, "Diary of a Conservationist", on August 25, 1955:

"There is considerable discussion concerning the twenty-six acre property of Rupert Edwards lying on Lawrence Avenue near the Leslie Street Extension. Mr. Edwards offered to sell the property to Metro for about $160,000, or a third of the amount the subdividers had offered him. The property has been beautifully landscaped. There is a water wheel in the Creek, (which I call the Milne Creek), on the site of the first Milne Woollen mill on the Don. I have since received a letter and clipping from the Municipality of Metro Toronto advising that a committee had recommended the purchase of these acres to be supervised by the township of North York."

About ten years after that item appeared in my column, I visited with Mr. Roy Belyea, then a Controller for the City of Toronto. Mr. Belyea was the owner of a plumbing firm on Merton Street. I was with the Metropolitan Toronto and Region Conservation Foundation, as well as the Authority, at the time. This connection with the greenbelt prompted him to tell me his story of Edwards Gardens. He said that he had negotiated the sale of the property to Metro with Mr. Edwards. The property was immeasurably valuable, whether it was used for estate housing development or for greenbelt and recreational purposes. Finally Mr. Edwards said to Mr. Belyea, "Very well, put my name to it and you can have the property for $250,000." When this was reported to Metro, a very prominent person, who I will not name, said, "Why you fool. You will never get a baker's dozen of people there." An opinion which seems unbelievable when one considers the popularity of Edwards Gardens today. When Mr. Belyea passed away I made an effort to ensure that there was some recognition for what he had done. To this end, my article on the incident appeared in several weekly newspapers, including the *East Toronto Weekly*. My clipping of the article has been mislaid but the figure of $250,000 sticks in my mind. Imagine buying Edwards Gardens for the price of a new suburban dwelling today!

Thousands of people who use the valley systems for recreation today do so in total unawareness that the land they are walking over was a gift from some distinguished citizens.

Metropolitan Toronto owes a debt of gratitude to wealthy families who, having preserved their Valley properties, either deeded them to the Crown outright or sold them at bargain prices. Examples of this are the Grant Glassco property in the Humber Valley; Heart Lake, the Edmund Boyd property at Woodbridge; Serena Gundy, Don Valley and Kilgour Sunnybrook Estates; and the Snively property at St. George's Lake. Other names could be added to the list and the number of people who pass on their estates for public use is growing.

175

The structure of parkland along the Don was confirmed in the *Globe and Mail* on June 20, 1967 in an article entitled "Metro's Miles of Wilderness":

"...It will be possible to walk from Lawrence and Bayview Avenues through 5½ miles of wooded valley to Victoria Park Avenue [later extended to Warden Avenue]... It is a virtual wilderness,... Wilket Creek Park adjoins Serena Gundy Park, named for the mother of Toronto businessman Charles L. Gundy, a bequest from the family estate... Northwest of Wilket Creek Park lies Sunnybrook Farm, bequeathed by Alice Kilgour, widow of Joseph Kilgour, a parcel directly behind more woodland acquired behind Sunnybrook Hospital on Bayview Avenue from the Federal Government. The Federal Government also turned over a plateau site of some unused Department of National Defence building, that connect Sunnybrook Park with Wilket Creek forest.

"South of Eglinton Avenue, Serena Gundy and Wilket Creek Parks join the wildest part of all... [west valley of the Don to Forks of the Don which now contains a wetland natural area]. Taylor's Bush Park lies across the Don Valley Parkway and railroad tracks. it is linked to Seton Park by a footbridge over the railway and by access under the Don Valley Parkway.

"Taylor's Bush Park curves in a crescent south of O'Connor Drive and St. Clair Avenue, running into Dentonia Park, a parcel donated by the family of former Governor-General Vincent Massey. This extends to Victoria Park Avenue... All this is right at the geographic heart of Metro."

It is appropriate here, having mentioned Wilket Creek in this chapter, to include here information that came to me through my life-long friend Harold Wills of the York Pioneer Historical Society. Wilket Creek, I felt, should have been named after the Milne family. However this is what Harold says about both Paul Wilket and Alexander Milne:

"Wilket Creek has been known by that name since at least 1818. Paul Wilcot owned lot 23, I conc. W. from 1805-1818: and Jonathan Wilcot owned lot 22, I Conc. E. from 1799-1816.

Paul Wilcot emigrated from Pennsylvania in 1793. He became Overseer of Highways and Fence-Viewers for Yonge Street from Big Creek Bridge (in York Mills Valley) to Steeles in 1799.

"Between 1820 and 1823 a substantial saw mill was built on Wilket Creek close to Yonge Street, on the northwest corner

of what is now Drewry and Yonge. The property originally belonged to John Mills Jackson of Jackson's Point, and in 1823 it was bought by George Playter.

"Up to 1860 Wilket Creek crossed Cummer Avenue just east of Yonge. Since 1960 it has crossed Yonge just north of Gibson House.

"Alexander Milne established a woollen mill in Don Mills in 1827. It was situated on Wilket Creek on the site of today's Edwards Gardens. Before that time he had carried on a carding and fulling business (along with a partner) in the flour mill of James Farr in Weston. From there he went to Markham and into partnership with a brother.

"He stayed on Wilket Creek only five years. In 1832, because of a dwindling water supply, he moved to a new location on the Middle Don River, south of Lawrence Avenue, east of Don Mills Road."

Before leaving the subject of Edwards Gardens, reference is made to a very old and huge apple tree still growing on the property. It was probably planted by the Milnes around 1795. However, when a nursery of pioneer apple trees was started at Vineland, I forwarded two dozen cuttings from this old veteran, where in all likelihood they were grafted to root stock to perpetuate their usefulness. Finally the Milne family burial plot adjoins the present Edwards Gardens parking lot on the south. An immense red oak tree still stands guard over the remains of the families who lived there when the tree had started growing.

One evening Fletcher Sharp called me. He said in flat tones, "I have been out for a ramble. It's gone, cleaned out, not a trace of it left." He had been walking along the Barber Greene trail when the woods had suddenly disappeared and there before him was a long wide trench made practically overnight for the Leslie Street extension. It looks much better today, with trees, grass and shrubbery enclosing the extension, but to a person to whom the woods had offered untold opportunities for study and recreation, their sudden demise was quite a shock. I sometimes wonder how many of those joggers whose legs carry them over the smooth macadam of the present trails in the Don Valley system consider how many heartaches lie buried in the same area. The making of the Leslie Street extension probably drove home to Fletcher Sharp the concerns of conservationists who had been fighting to save what could be saved of the Don and other valleys. As countless persons have learned, the natural scene that they love may some day have to be fought for. When writing these lines I leafed through three huge scrapbooks of newspaper clippings describing the battles that were fought to preserve the Don Valley. This is the major reason why so much of the Valley is still left.

Adieu Barber Greene woods, *adieu* the memories and the battles of yesterday. Everything seems to be so much in place today, the well-laid out parks, the nature trails, the transplanted trees, the groups of casual walkers. The tower of the Inn on the Park stands where we once rambled through fields of goldenrod. The IBM office and plant replace the turnip pits of Donlands Farm and the CPR locomotives no longer whistle the crossing at Don Mills Road because it too has disappeared.

Occasionally the Inn on the Park prepares picnic lunches for guests who are invited to use the park facilities to enjoy their food in a natural setting. I am sure at times some of these people from across Canada look up at the tree trunks and wonder how those battered metal signs, "Stop, Don't Cut Trees", were ever put there. Most of the people who nailed them there, like the scenery they tried to protect, have disappeared.

Along in 1980 Fletcher Sharp began gradually to fail. It was inevitable but heartrending, for I knew too well what lay ahead. Our outings were more casual now, carried out in a reminiscent mood. I would at times carry two folding chairs and place them so that we could look over the Valley and enjoy the sun and chat about how times were. He would then remind me of the things that had happened. "You remember when I asked you to imitate an American toad." This was near a pond by the railway at Vandorf. It was a drowsy, late spring day. The male American toads (*Bufo americanus*) were probably dozing in the warmth of the day. Suddenly my piercing trilling was carried over the closest pond. Immediately a male toad, sensing some threat to his domain, responded. His call awakened other toads in neighbouring ponds. When we left the toads were trilling across the countryside. Fletcher still chuckled as he remembered the incident.

There were a few more of these autumn outings, then suddenly it was all over. As he had often said to me when I asked how he felt about living his very long life, "So good to have seen it", which is saying a great deal.

Thus passed from my life as quickly as he had come into it more than 30 years before, one of the kindest, most considerate and helpful men it has been my good fortune to meet. In his own way he made his mark by exploring the Don Valley from his Rosedale home and sharing what he could share with others in his innumerable outings. Botanists and ornithologists are often held up to ridicule as nature freaks but here was one of the distinguished physicians of Toronto, incredibly busy in his profession, exceedingly knowledgeable in matters of scientific interest, finding the time and the emotion to fully treasure the natural scene that he found at his door. *Adieu* Fletcher Sharp, *adieu*.

CHAPTER TWENTY-NINE

Remembering the Don

My book, *Remembering the Don*, was one of the great surprises of my life. Its success was a revelation to me.

One book reviewer said the writing was inspired by a pure love of the subject. I had overlooked or underestimated the fact that my love of the Don Valley was shared by thousands of people. *Remembering the Don* recalled their own memories of the Valley. The Valley was not only the area from Queen Street to the Forks of the Don, but an arterial system with two main valleys, several sub-valleys and many spur or side ravines. A person traversing the Don River watershed could walk in several directions for 16 miles or more. People had lived along these Valleys, or their parents had farmed near them, or perhaps they had just known the Valleys as I had. But for whatever reason the Valley of the Don, or Valleys of the Don, remained ever fixed in their minds.

The publication of *Remembering the Don* was followed by a sustained stream of telephone calls and letters. One man said, "I cannot thank you enough for writing that book, for what it has done for me in recalling priceless memories." Another said, "Why, we lived at Donlands Farm. However did you put all that information together?"

So it went, and so it goes. Representative comments are grouped in the following chapter.

"While in Ottawa I spotted your *Remembering the Don* in a bookshop, much to my delight ... I read it from cover to cover ... Part of my appreciation is the result of my personal past contact with the Don, particularly with the Forks and Silver Creek. I grew up on Milverton Boulevard. My earliest recollections of contact with the Don were our boyish expeditions northward to Silver Creek (after risking a run-in with Billy Taylor, whose land we had to cross to reach the Valley). The Valley became a favoured outing spot to hunt crayfish and minnows, have a bare-bottom dip in the swimming hole at the white bridge, etc. In lean Depression years my parents and I would spend enjoyable leisure days up off Don Mills Road and I came to regard a trip across the Pottery Road to visit an uncle over on the west side as a mysterious encounter with the old buildings along the way . . . "

Wm. C. Wonders

"It took me about eleven seconds to get very interested in your book and head for the cashier . . . The book touches on people, events and interests in my own life of 60 years. I like the style and format too. It is an excellent book and one that I treasure. My address is the tall apartment building perched on the edge of the Don Valley overlooking the old de Grassi property. It's visible in the background of the picture taken of the de Grassi home on page 139 of your book . . . I was particularly interested in your knowledge of Ernest Thompson Seton. I was raised on him . . . I still have an aged and tattered *Two Little Savages* and *Wild Animals I Have Known* . . . Redruff and Silverspot were two favourites . . . I had spent time walking the Old Belt Line and finding the spot where the Moore Park Station had been, not knowing then that I was treading where Seton had spent much of his youth . . . As for the Forks of the Don area, I kept an eye on the old de Grassi place, had been inside it, phoned the Borough office whenever it was broken into and watched with anger when some vandal torched it a few years ago. Now it's all tidied up at the site in the usual fashion. Like the old paper mill (I've got some of its nails), the dam and mill pond, the old houses nearby, gone with hardly a trace. Not even a plaque. The Don even now is beautiful – if you overlook the dead water and get far enough away from the traffic's roar. In some areas one can still see it as the pioneers did. It must have been sad for you to lose it and see the desecration of two homesites . . ."

J.V. Cookson

"Your book has stirred many thoughts and emotions in me. In gratitude I would like to share my perspective on the Don with you. In 1934 my parents moved to 527 Donlands Avenue, just east of the Leaside bridge on the Valley. For the next 21 years that house and the Valley were home to me. Inspired by my father's interest in birds, my mother and I came to know intimately the south side of the Valley between the bridge and Todmorden Park . . . We often packed a lunch for an all-day excursion up the west branch of the Valley. No one could have asked for a richer environment in which to spend one's growing years. I remember your cottage with the large cardinal on it and wondered who lived there. Now I wish that we could have known each other. I remember attending the Don Valley Conservation

Association meeting one year (1951) at Fantasy Farm. I proudly presented my mother with a bluebird brooch that I won for correctly identifying a carving of a sparrowhawk by Frank Smith .... For some years now I have enjoyed dipping into a copy of *One Man's Harvest* left to me by my father. Inside the front cover is an inscription to my parents from you. I have enjoyed learning of the fascinating history of the Valley and relating your descriptions from the fifties to my memories. I wish to thank you for this book and your many efforts to preserve our natural heritage .... My interest in nature began on the Don .... Unintentionally, I find myself living a stone's throw from the headwaters of the east branch on Don Head farms ...."

Ian Sinclair

"My son brought me a copy of your book. I intended to glance through it ... two hours later I was still wallowing in nostalgia .... At the turn of the century we lived on north Sherbourne Street and from there straight into fields of daisies and wild roses (Rosedale?). We later moved to Crescent Road and I used to write about my son playing hookey from school in the ravine with Sonny McArthur .... So many familiar names: W.F. MacLean (my uncle Billy) .... It was a treat to visit Donlands. We would go to the corner of Broadview and Danforth to be met by someone from the farm, cousin Molly or Donny (Hugh John) to drive our horses Flash and Wolfbite. The house was not exactly a cottage, with a big dining room in the centre, a small room at each end leading into a big room. One was called irreverently "The Grandmothers Trap" for the floors were so highly polished. Behind the dining room was the kitchen with a Chinese cook ...."

Alice McKeys

[*Author's note:* The house was adjacent to the Canadian Pacific Railway line. In my day the fireplace and chimney were still standing. This would now be covered over by the Eglinton Avenue East extension.]

"I swam in the Clay Banks swimming hole, walked and learned about birds, collected wild flowers for school projects, slept under the stars in a blanket and had many wonderful hikes in the Valley. Sam Mayne was a friend of my father's. I spent many pleasant fall days along the hedgerows and fields of his farm. When the D.V.C.A. was formed, I was at the meeting in East York Collegiate. In later years after M.T.R.C.A. was formed,

I served on your Advisory Board. thank you for bringing back some beautiful memories with your wonderful book ...."

Dave Adair

[*Author's note:* The Maynes farmed at the top of the Valley on what is now Parkview Hills. They reached the farm by a road cut into the side of the Valley and which was reached by a bridge over Taylor Creek. The road is still visible.]

"From my earliest days with Lever Brothers I have understood that there were two main reasons why William Lever (later Lord Leverhulme) chose the site of the Lever factory on the east bank of the Don and south of Eastern Avenue. First, it was marshy ground and presumably could be acquired cheaply and, second, it was on a navigable stream which would be convenient for the receipt of raw materials, especially fats and oils coming from tropical lands. How interesting that your father came to Toronto to dredge the Don and presumably improve its navigability. However, so far as I know, water transport was never an important factor after the Lever plant was built around 1899.

"Incidentally, the land Lever bought originally extended up to Queen Street and in the early years of this century a park and playground was created for company employees called Sunlight Park, which was also used by residents in the neighbourhood. In later years everything north of Eastern Avenue was sold off .... As one who has lived for 25 years close to the Valley of the Don, or its tributaries, I have personally appreciated the natural beauty which still remains. That it does is largely due to your personal efforts and those of the conservation authority. You are to be congratulated for this effort and also for recording the history fo the Don."

R.W. Bates

"It was my good fortune recently to choose your book, *Remembering the Don*. I can't remember when I have enjoyed reading a book as I did while devouring each page of this .... My husband and I moved to our present home in 1950 – our four sons, as cubs and scouts, enjoyed many camps and hikes through what is now Edwards Gardens, Serena Gundy and E.T. Seton parks. In the early '40s I recall driving for a day's outing to what is now Sunnybrook Hospital area but which was wild, lovely country then, approached by Blythwood which was a gravel road. My sincere thanks for your efforts to keep the Don as I remember it, and also my appreciation of your book. I hope there will be another. Surely there are many more *Cardinal* anecdotes.''

Orvilla Miller

CHAPTER THIRTY

End of One Trail, The Beginning of Another

On June 23, 1984, during the Toronto Book Fair, an elderly gentleman stopped at the ticket booth. "Is Charlie Sauriol in there?" he inquired. "I am from Vancouver. I want to see him. We camped up the Don 60 years ago and I still have snapshots of those days."

I had not seen Art Kellythorn since he and his brother Jack, now deceased, carried haversacks, blanket rolls, pup tents, other scout troop paraphernalia and food along the railway track to the pine grove camping place, adjacent to the Don River and the Clay Banks swimming hole.

Art's visit unleashed a flood of memories of my one-time companions of the 45th Troop, some deceased, others whose whereabouts are unknown to me. I recall easily the names of several of them: Gord Collins, Reg, Jack and Ray Jeffs, Chuck Hester, Charlie MacKenzie, Kenny MacKenzie, Stan High, Jack Snow, Al Thomas, George Smith, Perc Parish, Lloyd Sloan, Kenny Brabant and Bill Nokes come to mind, and of course Art and Jack Kellythorn.

For several years after our camping days I saw these fellows at Troop reunions and sometimes met them on the street. To their credit, every one of them had become a citizen in good standing in the community. These were the young men whose uncles, father or older brothers had fought in the Canadian Army during the First World War.

Art Kellythorn, like many other boys of my time, never forgot the Don. Many a boy grown to manhood, who had also experienced camping up the Don, could tell of quiet pilgrimages made on visits to Toronto to see the old camping places once more and to meet some of the companions of those days.

Why, I have often asked myself, were they so drawn to the Don? It may have been that in a world that constantly hustled and bustled, the Don Valley had stood still, and this despite the scars left from being next door to a big city. It is today very much as it was when I first saw it. The boys of my generation may not have had any spectacular experiences along the Don, but they enjoyed a measure of freedom, the memories of which remained pressed in their minds all during their lifetimes.

The Severn River, at Severn Falls precisely, provides an example of the power of commonplace scenes to remain with us. Groups of the 45th camped there in 1924 and 1925 when there was not a boat on the river, just canoes. What a wilderness it was. To me these experiences are unforgettable to the point when, having looked at the old snapshots during the winter, I feel the urge, come spring, to get in my car and again visit the scenes of my youth. Progress has also visited the river, although the scenes of 1924 remained largely unchanged. The boat house where we picked up the canoes, the river as it flows under the Canadian Pacific Railway bridge and the pine and maple woods on the shore where we camped are all very much as they were.

The experiences along the Don and the Severn were the beginning of my career as a conservationist, during which I have been involved with the purchase and protection of tens of thousands of acres of natural area or heritage land. One would think that in the light of this experience there would be little place for memories of either the Don or the Severn. But through them I learned how important it was to save now every acre of green space that could be saved.

In June 1984 a friend showed me a house he had just bought. It was one of those houses largely indistinguishable from any other, but fulfilling the needs of its owner. These rows of houses have sprung up like mushrooms on the farm fields of a few weeks before, the last harvest that would ever be gathered from their rich soil.

As we drove back through the more settled parts of the city, I was saddened beyond words. Most of my generation feel the same way when they realize that the open countryside they had known is now beyond recall. While this is a fact of life today, there are breathing spaces. In my case it was still possible that evening to take a long walk up the Don, in an unspoiled oasis of green. On the following Saturday, I went to my bee yard, ignited fuel in the bee smoker and watched the nacrous sumac smoke drift like incense over the trees. There was scarcely a sound. I could have been a hundred miles north of the city. The fact of the matter is that people in Toronto do have their green spaces to go to. We are just beginning to discover the therapeutic value of the Don and other valleys.

The Don River no longer flows red, then a day later green or yellow from the dye of a paper mill as it did in the 1950s. Nor do I play trumpet with a brass quartet on my cottage lawn at the Forks of the Don as in 1929, for everything within that landscape, including the cattle munching grass on the other side of the fence, has long since disappeared. Nor do militia regiments shuffle back and forth in mock battles on the Riverdale Flats as they did at the turn of the century. Nor do the boys of the 45th Troop, heavily-laden with equipment, sweat their way in the July heat along the railway track to the pine grove camping place. This way of life, like so much else, has come and gone.

Gone too are the days of Chris Stong, who claimed he was the greatest coon hunter of all times, who caught raccoons in MacLean's sugar bush whose pelts provided fur coats that ladies no longer wear. Gone too are the days when stores along the Danforth were provisioned with vegetables grown at the foot of Tumper's Hill and in fields that adjoined the Valley at Eglinton and Don Mills.

At times, when I tread the old trails, I feel like one whose generation is slipping away. Sometimes I feel people are like trees, a thought prompted by these lines written by Dr. Henry Scadding, an early Toronto historian, in this eulogy to a forest of white pine trees that once grew near the site of Castle Frank:

> *"The last of thy sturdy race,*
> *Thy tale now tell to me,*
> *For sure I am it must be strange*
> *Thou lonely forest tree."*

Am I lonely? Perhaps, but never for long, for some of the past lives on in the present, if we have been able to make our mark on society. A visitor asked me, while I was working on *Tales of the Don*, if I could remember what I had done on June 20, 1936. I could not, but I checked my diaries, for I have recorded events there for more than 50 years, and through these entries recall other events of before that time. The June 20, 1936 entry included this extract:

> *"This bright, hot June 20th found me in Else's swimming hole.*
> *My first dip of the season over the piled-up sand bags that had*
> *raised the Don three and a half feet . . . what a treat! Else came*
> *along and we splashed about in great content. His cabin has*
> *a festive air through the petunia beds he has planted around*
> *it. Can this be the place where just a few months ago everything*
> *was deep in snow?"*

Thus through the diary I have at my fingertips a complete record of events of the time.

As I have learned, one train of thought leads inevitably to another. *Tales of the Don* was no sooner finished than a casual question directed to me raises the possibility of yet another book, bringing together those observations strewn throughout my diary pages of 50 years or more. Exciting, indeed, the prospect of rescuing them from oblivion to put before people who would not otherwise know about them.

In conclusion, it might be truly said, in the words of Robert Browning:

> *"Grow old along with me!*
> *The best is yet to be,*

The last of life, for which the first was made:
  Our times are in His hand
  Who saith, 'A whole I planned,
Youth shows but half; trust God: see all, nor be
  afraid!'"

Author out on a Winter hike, January 1948.

Charles Sauriol (1984). Author also of Remembering the Don and A Beeman's Journey. (Photo Sheila Clark).